WORKING FROM HOME

MAKING THE NEW NORMAL
WORK FOR **YOU**

WORKING FROM HOME

KAREN MANGIA

WILEY

Published by John Wiley & Sons, Inc., Hoboken, New Jersey.
Published simultaneously in Canada.

For general information on our other products and services or for technical support, please contact
our Customer Care Department within the United States at (800) 762-2974, outside the United States
at (317) 572-3993 or fax (317) 572-4002.

Wiley publishes in a variety of print and electronic formats and by print-on-demand. Some material
included with standard print versions of this book may not be included in e-books or in
print-on-demand. If this book refers to media such as a CD or DVD that is not included in the version
you purchased, you may download this material at http://booksupport.wiley.com. For more
information about Wiley products, visit www.wiley.com.

Library of Congress Cataloging-in-Publication Data is Available:

ISBN 9781119758921 (Hardcover)
ISBN 9781119758938 (ePDF)
ISBN 9781119758952 (ePub)

Cover Design: C. Wallace
Cover Image: Coffee Cup © Xacto/Getty Images
Author Photo: © Rogue Images Photography

Printed in the United States of America

SKY10020034_072320

To My Late Grandmother

Who Is Always Close at Heart

Contents

Foreword

I like to win.

As a kid, growing up in Canada, I knew I was born to race. I love to compete, I love to go fast, I love to say "yes" to life. And I was willing to do whatever it took to go full speed ahead toward my goal of competing in the Indianapolis 500.

Eight years of passion and persistence made my debut in the Indianapolis 500 in 2011 possible. Life was moving fast: I was recognized as the IndyCar Series Rookie of the Year. In 2012, I was voted Favorite Driver by IndyCar Series fans. Open-wheel racing was my new home. I was living my dream life at 230 miles per hour. I started 2015 with a new team. We won the Grand Prix of New Orleans in only our second race together. Things were going great. In May of that year, I was driving at Indianapolis once again. Race day at the Indy 500 was in my sights.

Until I came around turn number three.

That practice day started out like any other. The sun was shining, the track was clear, and I was working to perfect my car for the "greatest spectacle in racing." There was some light traffic and I was running behind a driver by the name of Montoya. I came into turn three at about 225 miles per hour. What happened next no one could have predicted.

In my business, I work hard to maintain perfection. To keep control. To make sure that I'm doing everything I can to keep that car going where I want it to go. But, in spite of my best efforts, something happened in the turn. Something beyond my control.

I don't remember exactly what transpired. The video shows that I was conscious after the crash, but I don't remember being in the car and bobbing my head as the crumpled chassis lay crushed on the pavement while the rescue crews came onto the track to pull me from the car. I learned about my new normal when I woke up in the hospital. I was hooked to machines and surrounded by family, friends, and doctors. I couldn't speak because of the tube down my throat. I had to communicate with a pen and a piece of paper. They told me what happened. And then I watched the videos.

In an instant, a piece of the suspension broke and pierced the chassis, sending me into the retaining wall. The accident was a mechanical failure. Probably some metallurgical issue that happened six months ago – who knows? – when the suspension was built 4,000 miles away from Indianapolis Motor Speedway. When the suspension failed, the car careened into the wall, forcing a metal shaft into my right thigh and striking my femoral artery on its way out of my left side. The piece that impaled me (that's a weird word to write about yourself) was connected to the car. Basically, I was a shish kebab.

In order to pull me out, they had to remove the metal shaft from my body – leaving a hole that my doctor said was big enough for him to insert his whole fist inside. Luckily, Indiana University Methodist Hospital was just a four-minute drive away – the police cleared the streets and the ambulance drivers told me they made it in 2:47. Not only was their speed impressive, it probably saved my life.

I had two complete blood transfusions before I even went into the operating room. My heart stopped. The doctors thought I would code before they could even get me into surgery.

Hey, let me stop for a minute. This isn't a foreword about an injury: it's a foreword about a recovery. Because that's what Karen's book is all about.

I realized that the only response to a setback is a comeback. If you're holding this book, right now, you know that's true. You're interested in getting back on track.

What's the fastest way to get back into a race car? I asked my doctor. He told me the thing I couldn't stand to hear: *Do nothing.* Can you imagine going from 230 miles per hour in your day job to an absolute standstill? To put it mildly: I didn't like it. But I did it. If I was going to do nothing, I was going to do nothing better than anybody. That's just how I'm wired.

Soon, my doctor told me I could try to walk again (yes, that's right: I had to be allowed to walk). That first day, they said I could only take a maximum – a maximum – of 600 steps. I listened to the five words I never want to hear: *"You have to start slow."*

Soon 600 steps led to 800 steps, and that led to physical therapy and a lot of other day-to-day stuff that was uncomfortable, difficult, grueling, and … well, everything you imagine it to be. They say in racing that you have to move slow to go fast. Now, out of the car, those words had never been truer.

Because trying to go faster is how most of us live our lives, right? Racing from one commitment to the next. From one thought to the next. Trying to shave seconds off every task in our own race against the clock. When you can't do what you used to do, because of unexpected circumstances, you don't want to go slow. But in order to make a comeback, you have to shift your mindset. You have to be open to seeing things in a new way.

There were two words that came into my life when I was in recovery. I said these words to my doctors, my family, and myself. I still do. Here they are: #ChallengeAccepted.

Life happens. The global pandemic happened. Nobody wanted it. Nobody asked for it. But, here we are. Challenge. Accepted.

We have to accept the challenge that life has given us. This book is going to give you the pole position on conquering those challenges. This book will give you a fresh perspective on the new normal. Karen will show you how to make working from home work for you.

In less than 18 months, I was walking, training, and driving better than before. Not only did I improve on everything I did before the accident, I also learned something new. I learned to dance. I became a contestant on the 2016 season of *Dancing with the Stars*. Did I ever think I would be doing the jive and the Viennese Waltz in front of a national television audience? Well, it was another unexpected series of events. I said, "Challenge accepted." My dance partner, Sharna Burgess, and I made it to the top two . . . but came in as runners-up. When one of the judges said I was the best male dancer they had ever had on the show, I was so grateful and honored and . . . blown away. I realized something in that moment: the past does not define us. Are you with me?

Today, I'm back to racing – I just ran at the Texas Motor Speedway in front of zero fans. And yes, it was strange. People ask me if I'm nervous when I get back in the car. I tell them that love is stronger than fear. I tell them that I can't let what happened to me keep me from being who I am. I tell them I want to win. Nerves, fear, disappointment, and surprises are part of the game of life. But so is victory. So is learning to dance in ways you never thought you could. Are you ready to get on the right track?

Life hands all of us unexpected circumstances. Luckily it also hands us courage. And passion. And the ability to choose how we react to whatever we've got. That's what Karen knows, and shares, in this book.

Getting back to work is hard in the new normal. Believe me, I know how that feels – we are all making adjustments and finding out what adaptability really means. Karen will show you how to adapt. How to shift into a new approach to success – because victory might be closer than you think.

Even when the unexpected knocks you out of the race, you can still bounce back. Even from a global setback. That's how human beings are wired.

It's time to start your engines. And maybe even learn some new choreography.

Something that may have started far away from where you are has forced you into unexpected circumstances. You find yourself in a situation that makes you say, "I never wanted this." You know what I mean?

I think we all do.

Through Karen's work, and her words, you'll see your path to recovery. Perhaps you'll even see that you are capable of much more than what other people might expect from you. You'll find your way to get up to speed again, no matter what your circumstances. Whatever race you're running, this book will show you how to find the confidence and innovation that you need. And maybe even try some new dance steps along the way. Reinvention is waiting for you. You just have to recognize that you are more than your circumstances. Are you ready to say, #ChallengeAccepted?

James Hinchcliffe

Professional race car driver, runner-up on Dancing with the Stars, *and the mythical mayor of Hinchtown (https://www .hinchtown.com).*

Entering the Shift

We are all shift workers now.

Working from home, under current conditions, is more than just a big change. The new normal is a shift for all of us, shifting from commutes and cubicles into a brave new world, where the line between work and home isn't just blurred – it's been erased.

COVID-19 has transformed the way that we work, interact, and live. But the change to working from home was happening long before the global pandemic. Post-coronavirus, much of work will not return to the way it was. And many workers won't be returning to headquarters anytime soon. As I write these words, it's difficult to predict what the new normal will look like exactly. Whatever the future holds, the odds are that you'll be looking at it from your home office.

This might be difficult to hear, but when the future is uncertain it's up to you to create it. To step into the shift, and thrive, you must create an environment that works for you. The change toward a remote workforce was already underway, even before Twitter and other organizations made the decision to make work-from-home a cultural norm:

- A recent Gartner CFO survey (https://bit.ly/wfh-Gartner1) reveals that 74% of financial leaders intend to shift some employees to remote work permanently.
- The same survey finds that 75% of CFOs plan to shift at least 5% of previously on-site employees to permanently remote positions post-COVID-19.
- Based on over 100 million data points from 30,000 users, Prodoscore (https://bit.ly/wfh-prodoscore) reports that remote workers are 47% more efficient than on-site employees: telephone calls are up 230% and Customer Resource Management (CRM) activity 176% in a post-COVID-19 survey conducted in the spring of 2020.

This book is about helping you to navigate these shifts, so that you can survive and thrive in a work-from-home world. My intention here is simple: to help you shift into the realm of success, so that you can be virtually successful no matter where you are. Because work is a thing you do – not a place you go.

Success is not a location. Neither is impact. Or personal branding. Or career management. Today, you can succeed from anywhere. You can make a difference from your kitchen table, if you want to. You can restart your career and reinvent yourself from your laptop – and this book will show you how.

As we move into a work world where the coronavirus has caused the biggest shifts in modern history, you (and your company) must adapt. There is no going back. Paraphrasing Robert Frost, the only way forward is through.

Adaptation requires a mindset shift. A cultural shift. And coaching that can help you to make the mindset shifts you need. That's where we are headed in the pages that follow. Specifically, I'm going to take you from adaptation to acceleration regarding your home office space. You'll learn how to turn video calls into powerful tools – and how to know when not to Zoom into a meeting. We'll go from challenge to change, as we learn from experts and top-tier organizations how to create a culture that adopts the new normal. Finally, we'll move from resistance to resilience, finding new ways to advance your career – even when your career is happening inside your home. Or you're trying to re-start one.

You've probably already realized that working from home takes different mental muscles than what you've been used to using. This book will challenge you to "work out" in new ways, so you can contribute without burnout. I'll show you how to address your home workspace with finesse, connect remotely with your entire team, eliminate Zoom zombie syndrome, and even deliver your best presentations ever. You'll learn how to manage multiple duties – from surviving in super-small spaces to managing a remote workforce of hundreds of employees. You'll be able to create impact for your customers, elevate your entrepreneurship, and more.

The good news is that working from home, ultimately, is *better*. Your journey has a great payoff for everyone involved.

That may be hard for you to believe as your dog starts to bark, your doorbell rings, and you've decided your two home-schoolers both deserve detention until 2026. Yet, through my involvement on the Work from Home Taskforce at Salesforce, I've seen one thing clearly: there is a better way to manage working from home. This book is designed to help you to find it.

And to find it on your own terms. I'll share my story with you – I've been working from home since 2002 – but this book isn't about my story, or even my solutions. It's about helping you to find yours. Because everyone has a different experience of what working from home looks like, we'll look at specific examples that can influence yours. Perspectives that focus on what really matters here: your success. Sometimes you find that perspective in the most unlikely places. I know I did.

"Here. This is for you," my aunt said, her tiny salt-and-pepper curls framing her silver-rimmed glasses. As soon as she had placed the box in my hands, my aunt turned to walk down the driveway. Strange that she would give me a gift as she was saying goodbye. "I want you to open it by yourself," she said, pulling on the car door. She paused to smile at me. "You'll know why."

The box was barely big enough to hold two decks of playing cards. I could tell there wasn't any jewelry inside it. The rectangle shape was wrong, the thickness didn't feel right. Forever the kid at Christmas, I shook it – no sound. The only thing I heard was my aunt driving away. What could it be? Back inside, I pulled the light blue bow. It came apart easily in my fingers. The package was flawlessly wrapped, with crisp folds and perfectly placed tape – a reminder of my aunt's methodical attention to detail. As I removed the paper and eventually the lid of the box, I could smell that faint cloud of nostalgia – as if a piece of an old library book had been placed inside. Turns out, I wasn't far off.

A small red hardback book was nestled inside the box. On the book was some gold lettering, unclear and mottled like an out-of-focus picture from days gone by. I brushed my hand across the cover. As I pulled it closer, the title became clear: *Another Chance*.

I opened the first page to see if I could discover who had written it. From the faded lines and careful penmanship, I realized what I held in my hands.

I was holding my grandmother's diary.

She had started writing it when she couldn't head off to university because of what was happening in the world.

The first entry was dated Friday, September 28, 1945.

As I flipped through the pages, a new image of my grandmother began to take shape in my mind's eye – like seeing the San Francisco skyline after the fog fades away. Inside the pages I met a bright young woman, trying to find her place in the world during a difficult time in history. She saw the global turmoil as a chance to begin again.

Going away to college was a dream deferred, due to the war. Her entries reminded me of the frustrated graduates from May of 2020, unable to go through a traditional ceremony because of social distancing restrictions. What does it mean if you can't go to school like you'd always planned, my grandmother had wondered.

She had to take a job keeping the books at a nearby lumberyard. She enrolled in classes at a local university extension, seeing somehow in the midst of disappointment a chance to reset. Perhaps even to head in a new direction.

She felt a lot like what you and I are feeling right now, I guess.

The world wasn't what she had asked for, but it was the world nevertheless.

As I held those yellowed pages in my hands, reading her words, hearing her voice from a century long past, I knew my grandmother in a new way. The writer of this diary wasn't the woman who had read to me as a child or who had baked my favorite cookies because I got a good grade. She was an intrepid soul who wouldn't let global conditions keep her from becoming who she was meant to be. Can you relate?

What's your diary entry, today?

Are you ready for another chance?

> **Vala Afshar** ✓
> @ValaAfshar
>
> It takes courage and humility to start over.

This is my pal, Vala. He inspires me. Maybe he will inspire you?

Some call this time, this COVID-colored world, the Great Pause. You and I are being handed opportunities to re-examine the boundaries that surround the things that really matter. And, yes, your work and your career really matter. We have a chance to redefine success, to reshape the future – even if that journey starts inside your home office. The question is: what are you going to do with your chance? Here's what my grandmother shared in her first entry:

> *I know I miss everyone. So I guess the real reason is that I'm just scared. I'm afraid I won't make good of it all. What after college ... will it be Frank? [Spoiler alert: it wasn't. Sorry, Frank.] Will it be someone else? What of the courses that I'm studying for? Am I headed off for a career right now? I'm going to write a letter to the people back at home. Oh, how I wish I were there.*

Are you feeling a little homesick right now? For some, that word has more than one meaning. Perhaps you're wishing for the way things were, which is the traditional definition of homesickness: longing for a place that's different than the one you're in now. Or maybe, for you, you're *sick of home.* Either way, you're spending time longing for something that was normal before but isn't right now. Because the future looks very uncertain. Believe me, I know the feeling. I hear you.

What is it that you're missing most? Your rituals? Routines? Boundaries? Quiet children and animals that won't interrupt your Zoom calls?

I wrote this book to point you toward the opportunity in what lies ahead. If I could, I would have titled it *Another Chance,* but Grandma beat me to it.

As I finished the diary, leaving her world to return to my own, I realized the wonderful gift that I had been given.

I realized that all the time that we spend looking in the rearview mirror, being homesick for what once was, keeps us trapped. Living in a context that's no longer relevant isn't useful, but we pine for the past when what's ahead makes us feel insecure. But even in the midst of global upheaval, there's still a chance to move forward. To go home, again, for the first time. And to remake your "home" on your own terms.

My grandma taught me that we can find that place – that future – when we know where to look. She showed me that in words I read long after she'd passed away. Through my aunt's mysterious gift, my grandma gave me a powerful understanding. That understanding was the theme of her diary:

You can always begin again.

You can always restart. There's always a new path, even if you don't see it right away. Whether you are an executive leader, entrepreneur, individual contributor, or even someone looking for ways to get back into the workforce: work-from-home is the best way forward. Whether one day a week or seven, the future of work has changed. Are you ready to change with it?

> "They always say time changes things, but you actually have to change them yourself."
> -Andy Warhol

There are a lot of ways to take this book in: one is as a how-to guidebook on how you can set yourself up for maximum productivity. Another is as a corporate blueprint for building a work-from-home culture one employee at a time. But ultimately, there's another story to be discovered: a story about your success. Your reinvention. Your ability to respond in new ways to the changes that are still happening all around us.

That's the story – the story of personal success – that I've been sharing with thousands of people, just like you, via my work at Salesforce and in my first book, *Success With Less*. Together with a talented team, I've been helping many people to transition successfully into the work-from-home world. Now it's time for you to write your own story – and to bring that story to life, from right inside your home office.

I invite you to take another chance. To take a fresh look at what it really means to make work-from-home work for you. Let's utilize the Great Pause as an opportunity to go in a new direction. To rethink your career and your contribution. To shift toward even greater success, in a work-from-home world.

Possibilities

Let's talk about your sweatpants.

Remember when the coronavirus hit? One of the biggest and most striking impacts, in many ways, was a loss of context. Sweatpants became the new work uniform. Here are just a few of the things that changed because the entire context of our lives was disrupted:

Going to school	Dining out	Going to a movie
Traveling to London	Dating	High school graduation

What else would you add to the list?

When it comes to your career, your home office is your window into the world. And, like any window you look out of, people can see inside.

At first it was kinda charming and even mildly hilarious to see senior executives get interrupted by kids or a dog's unapologetic need for affection. People were real! Authentic! Quarantined!

The days blended together and time got bent in weird ways. Sweatpants kinda sorta made sense.

But as time has rolled on, it's become clear that working from home isn't a surprise party. It's not a pop-up event or a phase that can be solved with a simple retreat to your couch for a few days. Working from home *is* the new normal. How you show up in your home office is your context for success. Your colleagues have upped their game – have you?

People have started to realize that taking an important meeting from a rocking chair isn't the best strategy for success. If you're rolling onto a call at your company looking like your pillow created your hairstyle and you're sitting in front of a pile of dirty laundry wearing a t-shirt that says "Uncontagious," how do those choices reflect your professionalism and commitment to results?

Maybe it reflects poorly, but that's the real me, you might say. Because your old sweatpants and bunny slippers are a great example of the new kind of balancing act that has to exist when working from home. You've got to be yourself, and the last thing I would ever say to anyone is to try to live a lie or fit into some corporate stereotype. Or any stereotype, for that matter.

"It's me being me – me being *real*," you might argue, fighting for those pants that you should have abandoned after your sophomore year in college. After all, you might say, what's below my waist is not on camera. "This is who I am and I've gotta be comfortable. It's my right to dress however I want and to show up on video calls however I want. You just don't get it!"

Which might be exactly what your boss says when you ask for a raise or a promotion.

Ultimately, what you wear to work is your business – who could argue with that? But this book isn't about what to wear – it's about how to win. It's about you showing up at your best so that you can grow your career. Isn't that really what working from home is all about? Being comfortable, real, and *productive*? You need all three to make your home office really work for you.

What was quirky and cute once upon a time now looks like you just don't get how this whole thing works. I hate to say it again but you need to hear it: Your home office is your context. It's your place of productivity and the centerpiece of your professionalism. In video calls, it shows  how you're dressed for your role – even if part of your costume doesn't show up. Afterwards, when the camera's off, the space you occupy fuels and inspires your contribution – or it robs you of your potential.

We're talking about your place of doing business. Your zone of control. Your signal to your supervisor and your peers and yourself about the level where you want to be. Get that: *your home office is a signal to yourself.* A living breathing symbol of how you feel about your work, expressed in your surroundings. Are sweatpants really your A-game?

Considering the 30 million-plus unemployed workers right now as I write this, doesn't it make sense to make sure you're making a mark for yourself? Your home office isn't just a makeshift solution – it's a business tool of the utmost importance.

I wouldn't bring dishes, mixing bowls, whisks, and pans into my home office and try to cook something. It's easy to see that my office space isn't the right place for that. What is your home office space designed to do? Whether you're working in a dedicated room or just a repurposed corner of your apartment, you owe it to yourself to get clear on the right tools for the job.

And, getting back to those sweatpants for a second: there's one thing about them that we can all agree on. Comfort is really important. You can work from your laptop, sitting in a second-hand chair, hunched over like a bell ringer from Notre Dame, in dirty sweatpants, and still get the job done. Fair enough.

The right context for your success is a home office environment that's both comfortable and productive – a place where you can be at your best. What you wear is ultimately your business. But is your business set up in a way that truly serves you? How long do you want to wait to get into a home office environment that, unlike those baggy sweatpants, really fits you?

Comfort Matters

Your home office shouldn't be your bed, but it should be just as comfortable. Because you're spending a lot of time there, yes – but also because you deserve it. You deserve a space where you can make things happen – not where you're wondering if you'll ever get a moment of privacy. I'm not suggesting you need to wear a tuxedo or evening gown to your next team meeting. But working from home is about *balance*. Comfort and professionalism can coexist, in much the same way that a home can be a very effective office. Want to get the balance right?

Then ask yourself this question: Does your home office inspire you?

Looking in the direction of success means shaping your environment toward your goals. When considering your home office, your surroundings are an extension of your work, your life, and your career. And you've got to have a space that serves you.

At least, that's what I learned from Shakespeare's sister. Do you remember her? Her name was Judith.

She had the same aspirations and sense of adventure as her brother, William. She had similar gifts – in fact, she had as much or even more talent than her sibling. But he rose to fame while she vanished into obscurity, trapped by expectations instead of expanding into her true potential. Are you familiar with the story?

Of course, Judith was a fictitious creation of Virginia Woolf, invented in 1929 in her most famous essay, *A Room of One's Own*. Without a room of her own, Judith's life remained in the shadows, unable to fulfill her destiny.

Hopefully you're not afraid of Virginia Woolf?

While Judith was a fictional character, Woolf's point remains a hard reality: a room (or even just an area!) of one's own is critical to success. If your space is not inspiring – a separate place where you can do what needs to be done – how are you going to be successful in working from home? Beyond the tactical decisions about which laptop you need or what camera to buy, let's go upstream for a second. Let's look at the strategic decisions that go into a room (or space) of one's own.

Your home office needs to be a distinct, dedicated area. If you're trying to manage your career from your bed or your couch, you're not thinking about this the right way. Double duty is deadly; a dedicated space – even if it's a small one – is crucial.

Boundaries are the key to your success. As Robert Frost said, "good fences make good neighbors." And fencing off an area for you to work – exclusively for work – is just good business. And trying to pull double duty in a space, or cut corners, can be disastrous – and painful.

Work is a guest in your home. It only shows up where it's invited. You control the invitation. If you don't want work creeping into your family time or your fun time, don't let it. A separate space (even a section of your space) is the first step. But don't stop there.

"Here's where it all started," Kendra tells me, pointing behind her. She's a thirty-something product manager living in a studio apartment in Manhattan. She leans forward and twists, so I can see the area in question: it's just above her left hip. Turns out, millennial back pain is actually a thing. Especially if you're confined to a cheap chair. "Not a good idea," Kendra explains, elaborating on how she started working from home: sitting in a dining room chair for 9 to 12 hours a day. She saw the error of her ways. Kendra ends our call by pointing to the newest addition to her small space: a highboy leather office chair that looks like a pillow on wheels. "Now I'm all set," she says, leaving her back pain behind her.

A Seat at the Table? Unnecessary

Some folks don't even require a chair. I know, because I'm one of them. In my home office, I have what's called a treadmill desk. Some might say I've decided to take a stand against sitting in a chair.

Here's why: it's been said that sitting is the new smoking. That's right. Sitting down all day seems harmless at first but it's actually bad for your health. Our bodies were designed for motion. Sit/stand desks allow you to get on your feet, aligning your body and getting your blood flowing in the way that even the most comfortable office chair never could. (For more cool tips on how to turn your office into a fat-burning machine, my blog post [http://successwithless.net/moving-body-mind] shows how to burn 800 calories and buzz through 300 emails at the same time.)

The treadmill desk looks exactly like it sounds: a simple treadmill – not nearly as big or elaborate as what you would see at the gym – sits in the corner of my home office. The treadmill is fairly small, but still gives enough room for a good stride. At the front, held up by two gray pillars, is an adjustable-height desk. The desk is wraparound style: looking at it from above, it's shaped like a kidney bean. There's an indentation in the center (so I can walk comfortably and be close to my laptop). On either side, small wings hold notepads, a water bottle, and other office paraphernalia. The most important thing, right next to my laptop, is a small table lamp. Because, in my line of work, I need to be seen and heard – just like you do. The treadmill desk gives me quick access to tools, right at my fingertips – plus, I can still hit my Fitbit goals and get in those 10,000 steps per day.

I'm also a big fan of multitasking, so walking while I type this chapter is just how I roll. (But never rolling faster than 2 mph, because that's the maximum speed. Turns out that anything faster than a normal walking pace can cause a misstep. Believe me, losing your footing is a lot worse than a typo when you're on a treadmill.) On a video call or delivering a virtual keynote, my world is at a standstill – I don't walk. But I'm still standing, because that's how I feel most comfortable delivering the kind of work that I do.

And did you know that you can get going on a treadmill desk for as low as $400? Since the desk contributes positively to health and wellness, you can qualify to use your Flexible Spending Account (FSA) or Health Savings Account (HSA) for the purchase. When I got mine, I experienced increased productivity, increased movement, decreased anxiety ... and a diminishing waistline.

I know that my choices may not be right for you, so don't read my experience or personal decisions as a prescription. I'm just describing the alternative that works best for me. So let me ask you: What's your alternative? What's going to make you feel productive and energized in your home office?

Whatever you choose, choose *comfort*. A comfort that inspires you – not one that shows what you slept in last night.

Because you can't be at your best working in your jammies.

Arianna Huffington (https://bit.ly/wfh-arianna1) explains why:

"I fainted from sleep deprivation and exhaustion," she shares in her book, *Thrive* (Harmony, 2014). The incident left her with a broken cheekbone and provided a painful inspiration for her next book, *Sleep Revolution* (Harmony, 2016). In it, Arianna asks us to rethink rest – a subject I wrote about in my first book, *Success With Less*. It's vital that we take a pause – a break – in order to see things in a new way. That powerful pause is vital when you're shifting from your home life to your work life. There's a shift, but your location doesn't change. If you're wearing to work what you wore to bed, you're missing a powerful pause. And a critical mindset shift for your success.

Arianna says that having specific clothes for a specific task is critical. Find something that you can wear when you sleep and only when you sleep, she says, because it's a crucial distinction that our brains need. In a COVID-19 world where boundaries have been blurred, setting up the right context is crucial.

"Something switches in our brains when we put pajamas on," Arianna shares, describing the cues and clues that our bodies need in order to slow down. "On my nightstand is a pile of books that have absolutely nothing to do with work. They're novels, poetry, and books about spirituality." She doesn't drink caffeine after 2 p.m., and finishes her day by writing down three things she's thankful for, in a gratitude journal. Again, the distinction between waking and sleeping is a model of best practices when working from home. "Slipping on sleepwear is a signal to our bodies: time to shut down." What signals are you sending to your body when it's time to get to work? And when it's time to step away? Strategically, clothing choices can separate one function from another – even when those functions occur in basically the same space.

Your office environment is where you will spend some serious time. Shifting into an environment that serves you best is a small price to pay when it comes to your career. Virginia Woolf was right: a room of one's own is ideal for your creative pursuits. But what if you find yourself in a small space?

Marisol is laughing at that question. She always looks fantastic on video – I've been a guest on her global Zoom sessions for the pharma company where she works. Basically, she's broadcasting at TV-station quality with impeccable form and professionalism – but she's not in a studio.

In a private video call, she's acting like she's got a secret – and I'm wondering if she's ever going to stop giggling. I had simply asked her to pan to her right and left, because I was curious about what her home office space looked like. "You know what?" Marisol asks me, "you would find that I am literally in the corner of my bedroom," she says, lifting her laptop and panning to the left to show that she is quite correct. Her broadcast booth is wedged into a corner. Beside her are some toys on the floor next to an overflowing laundry basket and what looks like a half-finished school project – something to do with lava, I'm guessing, from the mountainous shape and colors. In other words, her place probably looks a lot like yours – but she's dedicated a small area inside of it to creating big results.

"I hadn't noticed it before," Marisol says, swinging the camera back to its original position, "but when I take my laptop here and there and everywhere in my house, I suddenly make every place my workspace. When I spread work out all over," she says, catching her breath, "I can't go anywhere to get away from work. There's no delineation – no boundary." That kind of work situation – where work is anywhere, everywhere, and always on – is a real turn-off for office success.

Surround Yourself with Success

When you see me on a Zoom call, you'll notice that a black-and-white photo hangs inside a simple black frame on the wall behind me. It's a picture of Maxwell Street in Chicago circa 1938 – a reminder of a special time, of someone who was very special to me.

As a little girl, I sat at the feet of my grandmother, listening to her tales of the magical market that lit up the short three blocks known as Maxwell Street – a place of wonder and fascination from her childhood to mine. What do you have around you that reminds you of who you are? Of where you've come from? Of the people who've gone before so that you can be who you are?

Hang pictures that inspire you. Mementos. Artifacts. Small items no bigger than a shot glass or ones that are as big as a motorcycle – whatever it is that feeds your soul and fits into your space. Place items nearby that remind you of what you've done – or to spark what you're going to do. We all stand on the shoulders of so many who have paved the way before. Who are those people, for you? In your home office, your choices are truly your own. The history, hopes, and dreams of my family and friends are a source of inspiration and comfort on every kind of day.

On my desk, in front of me, I see the box of cards from my three goddaughters. They wanted to inspire me while I was writing this book, so they sat down and wrote about 50 handwritten notes. (You'll have to check out my next book, *Listen Up!* [Wiley, 2020], if you want to meet the most amazing three girls on the entire planet, https://tinyurl.com/wfh-listenup. But I digress.)

When I'm feeling a little low, or a little quarantined (are you with me?), I reach into the box for a fistful of encouragement. I just pulled one out. The envelope is addressed to me, so it's like a miniature present with my name written under a big red heart. Like all of the cards, it's unsealed for easy access. This note happens to be from Lorelei (she won the Most Likely to Become a Leader award, at her virtual sixth grade graduation): "Don't give up!" it says, in multi colored markers, with a revised "e" next to a big exclamation point. She's not afraid to be bold. I like her style. "I am very proud of you and proud that I know you. So don't lose hope. – Lorelei"

How awesome is that? I'm lucky to have an entire box of inspiration right here on my desktop. Hope by the handful. How about you? What picks you up when the workday gets you down?

What is in your field of view, right now, that encourages you? What reminds you of who you are – and pushes you toward who you are yet to be? Surround yourself with the mementos and reminders that reflect your heart, so that your mind can function more effectively.

Building Blocks: Making Your Space Productive

More specifically, here are some clear-cut do's and don'ts, designed around a home office environment where video calls are part of your daily bread:

DO: Look here. Figure out a way to raise the camera on your laptop up to the level of your eyes. A shoebox or even a stack of books can help. From a nonverbal standpoint, we use eye contact to convey warmth, connection, and trust. How can you send that message without looking into the camera? Remember the old-school networking strategy: "Look 'em in the eye." The camera is where your audience is – keeping the camera at eye level will help your impact on every possible level.

DON'T: Have a stare-down contest. If you leave your laptop in your lap, or stare down at it on the table, you'll be broadcasting like Nostrildamus. I'm not talking about the sixteenth-century futurist and author of *Les Prophéties* (the prophecies). His name was *Nostradamus*. I'm talking about a twenty-first-century goofball, broadcasting nothing but nostrils to the boss and co-workers. I predict that nobody wants to see that. You don't have to be a prophet to know that a nose cameo could limit your future prospects at the company.

DO: Look for your light. The best light is natural and comes from a window in front of you. If you don't have a window in your space, place a lamp in front of your face so that you can be seen clearly. Ideally, it's a ring light or something that throws even focus onto your features. Want to find the best light, in any room? You need to do the Hokey Pokey. Let me explain: turn your smartphone into selfie mode and slowly turn yourself around. You'll see where the shadows grow – and where they go – as you spin. (If you want to put your left foot in, and then your left foot out, I'll leave that up to you.) Ideally, place your camera so that a good light source is in front of you – the source you identified in our hokey experiment. And let's just be honest: nobody likes seeing themselves on camera (we'll talk more about that when we discuss Zoom zombie syndrome a little later). But here's the deal: your face is the point of connection and expression, when it comes to making work-from-home work for you. If you don't care about how you look, you won't find your lighting. How will people find your ideas and your contribution if you can't be seen? So, you'll send a message of carelessness to all of your peers and co-workers. Just consider what kind of reflection that will make on your career.

DON'T: Play in the shadows. If you've got a massive light source behind your head, you're going to be sharing in silhouette. Why do that to yourself and your co-workers? Being backlit is the quickest way to invite your teammates to amateur hour, as your shadow work takes center stage. You've got to be conscious of what your lighting is doing to help or hinder your success.

DO: Consider your background. Piles of laundry and shelves of books behind you? You're inviting more distractions as people try to understand why you've got a copy of Vin

Diesel's autobiography on your shelf. If you've made it this far, you realize that your home office needs to strike a balance between self-expression (the items that say who you are) and self-distraction (those odd figurines and mementos are creating questions for folks – are those the kinds of questions you want?). If your background creates a barrage of bizarre inquisition, adjust your settings (starting with the setting behind you). When what's in the frame reflects unnecessary details of your personal hygiene, hobbies, or interests, there's a quick fix: *make a change*. You don't have to change who you are, just take some time to consider what's behind you! I'll say it again: your home office is your new context. That camera on your computer is a window into your world. Settings matter. Set your stage for your best possible performance, so you're not upstaged by your surroundings.

DO: Put on those headphones. Whether wired or Bluetooth, headphones are the quickest way to improve your audio quality. That way, there's little echo when you speak and outside noises (like the lawnmower right outside your window) aren't on equal footing because you're on the laptop equivalent of a speakerphone. What you have to say is important, but so is listening. Good headphones can make for a great start. As anyone in the video production business will tell you, "Good video is good audio." And if you're going to rock your presentation (that chapter is coming up), you've got to have a way to be heard. If you want to trick out your audio and your setup even further, you'll love reading about the guidance in the presentation chapter – where Hollywood producer Brant Pinvidic shares how you can quickly pump up the volume on a killer setup (without killing your expense account).

DON'T: Come on a group call unmuted. Don't be the person who shows up like it's the first time you've ever used Zoom. If you're in a noisy spot, where dogs are barking and phones are ringing, you're going to play the fool instead of making an impact. Learn where the "Do Not Disturb" setting is on all of your devices, and use it. That way, the bells and pings from email won't interrupt your calls. It's tough being interrupted in any conversation – but when you're interrupting yourself, as well as the 45 other people on the call, what does that say about your skill set? Not much! How about your ability to function effectively in this brave new online world? "I've got things well under control," the leader says, as his phone burps, his email jingles, and his dog bites the cat while the doorbell rings. Yikes! You need to learn how to turn down the noise in your home office – starting with the mute button on your favorite video call platform.

DO: Understand that interruptions will happen! Whether it's that huge presentation where your internet goes out or that tiny person who comes in crying and needs a hug, everyone knows that life happens. The question is, how will you respond when it does? I hope you squeeze the people who need a hug (work will still be there for you) and that you have a backup plan when the power blows. Think through how you will respond when life gets in the way of your sacred space – because part of making that space sacred means realizing that your office is also your home! Accept what comes into the scene, don't ignore it – or everyone on the call will lose their mind, as well as their respect. Have you seen the memes of the dad who ignores his kids, when he's on a video call? It's not a good look. Learn what great presenters and performers know: *be in the room, first of all.* Don't deny or ignore that enormous Maine Coon cat walking across your keyboard – we can see that thing and man, it's huge! But pet that cat and send it to friendlier confines, so that you can focus on what really matters.

DON'T: Make missteps a habit. If you're going to broadcast with a beefy snoring bulldog as your background, you've got to realize that Mr. Snuggles's respiratory challenges are a massive distraction. You may find his sleep struggle charming, but is it professional? Plus, who wants to be upstaged by Mr. Snuggles's snoring? Part of claiming your space is letting pets, people, roommates, and others know what's what when it's time to work. Sure, life happens from time to time. Dogs can fall asleep almost anywhere. But when you make a habit out of letting interruptions rule your world, it's as if you just aren't aware of where you are. There's nothing charming or cute in lacking awareness. Tune your EQ to your surroundings and make sure you see what's going on around you. Because what you think is cute can be annoying – and repeatedly allowing the same goofs to appear makes you look unaware and uninformed. What can you do, or say, to help others understand what you need? And is there a place where Mr. Snuggles might feel more comfortable during the video call? (Word on the street is that Mr. Snuggles is a good boy – I bet he'll understand.)

And if you really want to change the world, start off by making your bed.

That's what Admiral William H. McRaven (https://bit.ly /wfh-mcraven) told graduates at the University of Texas. It's a speech that still resonates – a reminder of how the small stuff can start you on the path to greatness. In a world where office boundaries have been shattered, time has been bent, and your home office environment matters more than ever, consider how his words might shape your context:

Every morning in basic SEAL training, my instructors, who at the time were all Vietnam veterans, would show up in my barracks room and the first thing they would inspect was your bed. If you did it right, the corners would be square, the covers pulled tight, the pillow centered just under the headboard, and the extra blanket folded neatly at the foot of the "rack" – that's Navy talk for bed.

If you make your bed every morning you will have accomplished the first task of the day. It will give you a small sense of pride, and it will encourage you to do another task and another and another. By the end of the day, that one task completed will have turned into many tasks completed. Making your bed will also reinforce the fact that little things in life matter. If you can't do the little things right, you will never do the big things right.

And, if by chance you have a miserable day, you will come home to a bed that is made – that you made – and a made bed gives you encouragement that tomorrow will be better.

If you have a tough day at work, your space reminds you (like a well-made bed) that tomorrow can be better. And you can shape your world, every day, to make it so. To make your space inspiring. To make your work world separate and special and productive. Take time to change out of your sweatpants and make your bed. These small steps can make a big impact – and build the context you need for success.

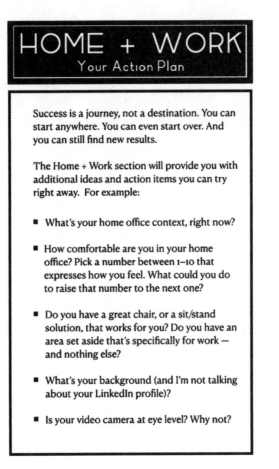

HOME + WORK
Your Action Plan

Success is a journey, not a destination. You can start anywhere. You can even start over. And you can still find new results.

The Home + Work section will provide you with additional ideas and action items you can try right away. For example:

- What's your home office context, right now?

- How comfortable are you in your home office? Pick a number between 1–10 that expresses how you feel. What could you do to raise that number to the next one?

- Do you have a great chair, or a sit/stand solution, that works for you? Do you have an area set aside that's specifically for work — and nothing else?

- What's your background (and I'm not talking about your LinkedIn profile)?

- Is your video camera at eye level? Why not?

Rituals, Routines, and Boundaries

Your laptop is your pantry.

When you're working from home, it's always there. Always available. Always tempting you. Like those pretzels or potato chips or donuts right there in your kitchen, work is always available if you want it. But you know that always grazing isn't a healthy strategy for your diet. It's also unhealthy if you're always peering into your work pantry.

Just because you *can* do something doesn't mean you *should*.

When work is always on and easily available, it's vital that you create some healthy segmentation – a separation between work and home.

You've got to close the pantry door.

To me, the key to success here is about being purposeful. Rituals, routines, and boundaries exist whether you choose them or not. For example, is banging out emails from your bed at 1 a.m. really your most productive time?

Maybe. Maybe it's the only time you've got. Hey, I've been there. But I've been there enough to know that no, crunching emails and working in the wee hours of the morning isn't really productive. Sometimes things bubble up, but is making a habit out of working all the time sustainable? Helpful? Desirable?

"Your calendar bleeds from one thing to the next and you check your email or feeds in between," says John Taschek, Senior Vice President of Market Strategy at Salesforce (https://bit.ly/wfh-sf1). "The fluidity of the day may be exciting, but you also may not be as effective as you think." When I note that he didn't mention taking time to feed yourself or take in fluids, he laughs. Seems like he's been there before – have you? "You may feel guilty for eating lunch so you do it in your home office area while casually listening in on a conference call."

Ultimately, this book is about helping you to be at your best – to turn your virtual world into a career powerhouse by building the habits that create success. Whether we realize it or not, humans are creatures of habit. What habits are you cultivating in your home office? How are your routines and rituals helping you to practice success?

Let's face it: working from home can be exhausting. You may not even see why, at first. Gianpiero Petriglieri, an associate professor at Insead, explains the dissonance that comes from video calls, when your entire work world is virtual. "Our minds are together when our bodies feel we're not. That dissonance, which causes people to have conflicting feelings, is exhausting. You cannot relax into the conversation naturally," he says in an interview with the BBC (https://bit.ly/wfh-fatigue).

Video calls require more focus than a face-to-face chat, because we can't always see all of the nonverbal cues we're used to. Body language comes in incomplete sentences. It's harder to process facial expressions and tone of voice. Research shows that delays of 1.2 seconds via video will make people perceive a responder as less friendly or focused, when it's really just their internet connection!

Marissa Shuffler, an associate professor at Clemson University, tells the BBC (https://bit.ly/wfh-fatigue) that part of the stress comes from performance anxiety – a natural stressor that shows up when you're always confronted with your own mugshot in a video call. "When you're on a video conference, you know everybody's looking at you; you are on stage, so there comes the social pressure and feeling like you need to perform. Being performative is nerve-wracking and more stressful." Seeing yourself, especially in back-to-back meetings, is a sure-fire recipe for self-consciousness. It's a shift from an in-person meeting, where (thankfully) I can't see myself when I'm talking with you. Want a quick way to reduce stress? Find the button so that you can hide your own image. Problem solved!

Staring intently at a person's face when you're talking to them just isn't natural. On a video call the only way to show we're paying attention is to look at the camera, according to the *Harvard Business Review*. But in real life, how often do you stand within three feet of a colleague and stare at his or her face? We are used to casually looking at the person we are talking to, not seeing dozens (or even hundreds!) of faces gazing intently at us. Researchers at the University College London have studied gaze duration – that is, there actually is a science around staring, and it's alive and well in the UK.

While researchers found that people are happy to stare at people they feel comfortable with for longer periods, looking intently at someone for more than three seconds is typically uncomfortable, especially when you're in a meeting with your boss, or your team. While you're just being attentive, your gaze might get misinterpreted.

It's all happening at once, Petriglieri says. Every interaction happens via Zoom, or some other online video platform, and that can be confusing. "Most of our social roles happen in different places, but now the context has collapsed," says Petriglieri. "Imagine if you go to a bar, and in the same bar you talk with your professors, meet your parents, or date someone; isn't it weird? That's what we're doing now.... We are confined in our own space, in the context of a very anxiety-provoking crisis, and our only space for interaction is a computer window." He calls the problem "self-complexity" – where everything happens via video calls. Everything, it seems, except variety.

All the more reason to establish boundaries and create separation in your home office, so that your online world doesn't become a jumbled mess of insecurity and confusion. And, in an upcoming chapter, we'll come back to the virtual world of video conferencing – with powerful ideas for improving your impact and conquering the challenges that pop up when your work world comes in through a single window.

But first, let's get back to finding a better way to work; video calls are just one aspect (albeit a huge one) that we'll cover in more detail later. First, let's explore some of the other challenges that can keep you from finding success, particularly when trying to conquer your calendar. Working from home requires a deliberate design around your schedule – those boundaries are essential to your long-term success. Many rituals and routines change when your home becomes your workplace. For example:

1. **A Strong Start:** When you go to the office, you have a get-ready routine because you have to be somewhere, dressed a certain way, and ready to work at a certain time. What happens if this habit doesn't carry over to your home office? When your commute changes from 60 minutes to six steps, it's easy to fall out of a standard routine. But business is a process: working from home is a process as well. What can you do to be purposeful about "going to work" when you don't have to worry about traffic on the highway and you can literally roll out of bed and log in to emails? As human beings, we need a break – a change – that's a deliberate signal that we are shifting into

a different mode. What's your going-to-work routine when you're working away from the company office? If you don't have an answer right now, find one. Don't leave your career to chance – don't freestyle your way to success. Establishing a schedule is the first step in setting the rituals that matter.

2. **Are We Done Yet?** When working at your company, the prompt to leave that office was likely something like beating the traffic. Or picking up the kids from daycare, letting out the dog, watching your soccer star play in her latest game ... you get the picture. As I write these words, all of those reasons have evaporated – except the dog. Dogs don't evaporate, and they still need to be let out. But letting your dog out the back door doesn't involve driving home from work. You depart and rejoin your life and interests much more easily right now – and whatever commute you were experiencing before actually has evaporated. Disappeared. Consider folks (like me) who would routinely drive to the airport and fly to various locations, some of them international. Or think about the cities with the longest commutes in the USA. According to CNBC (https://tinyurl.com/wfh-commutes), four of the top 10 are in California, with cities in the New York metro area rounding out the list. Jersey City, for example, has an average round-trip commute of 73.6 minutes. All of the top-10 cities boast commute times of over an hour. Now, those commuting hours have been returned. Are those minutes a gift, or a curse? According to Bloomberg, people are reporting that they are working an average of three more hours each day (https://tinyurl.com/wfh-bloomberg). Maybe that's because of managing home-schooling schedules. Or maybe it's just because the pantry is nearby. An executive at Intel reports clocking 13-hour days, working from home – and another says he has to set an alarm to remind himself to stop and eat. Are you managing your time, or is time managing you? Being deliberate about how

you use your time – especially time that's been returned to you – is critical to your success. Believe it or not, you can always make more money. But you can never make more time. Choose wisely: align your time in a way that's deliberate. That way, you establish new routines that help you to take advantage of what you've been given.

3. **Old School versus New Knowledge:** Remember the old days, when you would listen to a podcast, or call your mom, or just maybe listen to your favorite Spotify playlist on your drive home from work? What about driving from work straight to the gym, or maybe going to a happy hour meetup somewhere? These transitions signal your brain to transition from work – to change the channel and give your mind permission to leave work. What are you discovering as the new transition? Because you need one if you are going to be successful at working from home. Putting in long hours and pumping out great execution means building in the breaks that make the time more productive. Think about listening to music for a second: I've always loved music, and I often sit down and play piano to help myself decompress. But you know what I see every time I look at a piece of sheet music? A lot of white space. Without a pause, music is just noise. The rests in music aren't signs that the composer is being lazy – it's the composer being smart. The space is what matters as much as the notes! The pause makes room for what's new. For discovery. For connection. For change. Working from home asks you to compose your life on your terms. Have you built in the pauses that you need? Imagine a composer saying, "This melody is so awesome, I'm just gonna keep the sound going without a break for three minutes and people will love it!" No. No, they will not. That's not a song, that's just an unwelcome and haphazard racket. Frank Sinatra sang it best: "Without a song, the day would never end." Ask

yourself this question: where does the music come from? Is it just the notes, the words, the melody … or something else? Hear how the pauses make the music meaningful. Put those pauses back into your day, if you want a break from the noise. I know I do. Sometimes just taking a walk around the block is exactly what I need. How about you? Maybe tonight's the night you surprise your significant other with a dance party before making dinner together. (May I suggest you dance like no one's watching?) Or reading a chapter in a book (you're already off to a fine start, I commend your excellent taste). Others meditate or write in a journal. There's no right answer here, so choose the powerful pause that suits you best.

4. **Insights into Peak Performance:** What every high-performance athlete knows is that periods of peak performance require periods of peak rest. Jim Loehr, author of *The Power of Full Engagement*, studied the intersection between high-performance athletes and high-performance executives (https://bit.ly/wfh-meetjimloehr, https://bit.ly /wfh-meetjimloehr). "Balancing stress and recovery (https:// bit.ly/wfh-prioritize) is critical not just in competitive sports," he reveals, "but also in managing energy in all facets of our lives."

    "We live in a world that celebrates work and activity, ignores renewal and recovery, and fails to recognize that both are necessary for sustained high performance." He continues, "Energy, not time, is the fundamental currency of high performance."

    How well are you managing your currency?

5. **Divest Before You Invest:** In my book *Success With Less*, a story about an important promotion reminded me about how balance works. Have you been there?

Earning a promotion was important to me. And I had been work-ing toward the promotion for years. So, I invested.

Not only did I invest, I over-invested. Nights. Middle of the nights. Weekdays. Weekends. No hour was too late. Or too early. No slide deck was too elaborate. No voicemail was too detailed. No email was too lengthy.

I ran full speed into a burning blaze of activity every single day. Without hesitation. No matter how I might get burned or fully consumed at every moment.

Because I overlooked one important safety procedure.

Divest.

When you invest in something new, you must divest of something else. To make room in your schedule and in your mind to make the most of your new path. When I chose to invest in the high stakes project at work, I failed to divest of any of my other responsibilities. Inside of work. Or outside of work.

When you fail to divest before you invest, you lay the foundation on which to build damaging stories. And habits. "I have to keep all the plates spinning!" "I'm sure I can do it all if I just try a little harder!" "I don't want to be seen as a quitter!" "I'm so busy that I must be important! And successful!"

Back-to-back video meetings have suddenly become the new routine. Beyond the warnings from the experts, let's bring it back to a personal question: Is that always-on routine serving you? Putting you at your best? I assert that most people do not have a clear definition of what success looks like at work, and rarely have a sense of how they're spending their time.

Time shifts when you work from home. One moment flows into the next, am I right? Without the breaks and separation we have been taught to expect, the flow of the day can seem over-whelming – or invisible, until it isn't. Until you realize you're exhausted, but all you've done is sit in Zoom meetings all day. You've become a Zoombie – a walking zombie – as a result of too many video calls.

The first step in breaking the pattern, so that you can maintain your energy and sanity? Build rituals, routines, and boundaries so that you step out of the time warp.

When what we expect has changed, we have to adjust our expectations as well. Working from home is not the same as working in an office. Being online and plugged in and video-call ready at all times can be stressful – but it doesn't have to be. Inserting breaks will keep you at your best. Just as you structure your work space, structure your day and your calendar so that you aren't always on. I learned the hard way about how charging and driving and striving isn't the path to success – it's the fast track to burnout. Set up a space and a system that serves you, so that you have the separation you need in your remote work environment.

Before your calendar converts into chaos (a place where your pantry is always open), here are three quick and powerful questions you can ask yourself regarding any priority:

1. Does it have to be?
2. Does it have to be me?
3. Does it have to be me right now?

The challenge that can arise in working from home is based on a common maxim: if everything is important, then nothing is. Working from home, especially during the early days of the coronavirus, meant that many people had to handle homeschooling, video calls, new customer demands, explosive news reports, and more – all of it falling into the category of "overwhelm." Everything seems to demand your attention, and that causes burnout faster than you can say "change the channel."

You see, we need filters in our lives. Even when you're socially isolated at home, you still need a good filter to keep

Does it have to be?

Does it have to be me?

Does it have to be me right now?

out the stuff that you don't want. I'm talking about filtering out the noise and the obligations that don't serve you. What are the filters that will help you control your calendar, not the other way around? Those filters need to be built into your routine.

What if you could build your work-from-home world so that your days were more productive and inspiring than the office ever was? It's possible. In fact, it's probable: Success isn't reserved for someone else. Reading this book means you're interested in how to win the home game. Which means I like your style.

Maybe you've experienced some of the upside of working from home – finding yourself incredibly grateful that you don't have to jump on a train or fight the traffic. Realizing that you don't miss getting frisked by the TSA before you board your flight. Understanding that you never really enjoyed renting cars and getting lost in Portland. Or is that just me? Traveling isn't going away, but how we go about it is part of the new normal. We reinvent what that means, every day. That means that we are experiencing an unprecedented opportunity for creativity. You are creating your space and your calendar and your work-from-home world. Why not design it for the best possible outcome?

Work from Home: Exploring Perfection

Wonder why you never have a perfect day? Maybe you don't believe in perfection. As the saying goes, no one is perfect, not even a perfect fool. But haven't you ever said, "This is perfect"? Whether it's your partner or a pizza or a presentation, have you ever felt that shimmer inside that says "perfect"? Perfection does exist, when it's personal – we define it on our own terms. So, let me ask you a personal question: Why haven't you found your perfect work-from-home day?

Maybe it's just because you haven't taken the time to write out what it looks like. Take a moment, right now, and just consider: describe a perfect work-from-home day. **Create the timeline and the script.** Open up a Google doc or grab a pen and paper – take the time to explore what you really want. Otherwise, how are you going to get it? If your perfect day were a scene in a movie, what would it include? And if you were the leading actor in this drama, what elements would you bring to your performance? Be sure to consider other characters, props, and setting –that's your home office – inside this cinematic masterpiece.

Even in your perfect day, you've got to leave room for the unexpected! Fires and unpredictable events are a part of *every* day, so what's going to be different on a *perfect* day? The answer might be found in how *you* show up. After all, it's your performance that makes this movie a hit.

How would you fight fires and handle the unexpected, if you were truly at your best? Once you establish your home office, the scene is set. You've got to take the next step. You know what it is? Action! You've got to make your new space work for you.

The scene is ready for you. Now, on this perfect day, I wonder: Would you show up a little differently? How would you perform your role?

In the wild world of work, sometimes my circumstances are crazy, and I am surprisingly calm and productive. Other times, there's not a lot going on and I am kinda frantic, lost in thought and wondering which way to turn. Have you been there? Where your circumstances and your mood don't seem to mesh?

Being better than my circumstances is something that I have turned into a habit. That's not to say that I'm perfect or that I never get lost in my own head. I do. Believe me, it's been a lot of trial and error over the years (be sure to check out *Listen Up!* for some serious and candid straight talk about what I've had to process in my life). But when I'm confronted with opportunity, there are two words that have really opened me up to new possibilities. Two words that have helped me to see beyond my own thinking. Two words that I regularly share with my team as often as I can. Here they are:

"Why not?"

Those two simple words have unlocked more possibilities than I could have ever imagined. Because those words help me to break through boundaries and see the limits in my own thinking. As the saying goes, "It's never tougher than it is in your mind."

When I remove the boundaries that don't serve me, it's amazing what can show up. Challenges are everywhere: I make up stories and elaborate reasons inside my own mind why something is impossible. Have you been there? Isn't it amazing how many times we have conquered the impossible?

The first step in conquering the impossible, I have found, is a change in perspective. Want to redesign your work-from-home world? Don't think about why you can't do it! Ask yourself, *why not?* Want to advance your career, make an impact, find a new job or (let's go big) fall in love again? Right out of the gate, I bet there's a story you're telling yourself, and it doesn't have a happy ending.

Hey, what if you drop the story and replace it with two simple words? I love Simon Sinek's book, *Start with Why*. But when it comes to the new normal, I prefer starting with *Why Not?*

If you're a corporate leader and you're struggling with the idea that people can be effective when working remotely and it looks impossible for you to manage your team, stop for a moment. Is there a way to look at it through a

different lens? Why not? Why couldn't the team be effective and make progress and create results and expand your market share? Perhaps you're using yesterday's business model to create tomorrow's results. In the coming chapters you'll meet some executive leaders who are figuring things out in some innovative ways. But before we go there, let's consider where we are right now.

The coronavirus has been a cultural catalyst. The pandemic has accelerated the future of work. The new normal is filled with something known as VUCA – volatility, uncertainty, complexity, and ambiguity. The term first appeared in 1987, based on the leadership theories of two USC professors, Warren Bennis and Burt Nanus. While VUCA describes our times, the question remains: How will you adapt to them? The first step is removing the boundaries that point you toward what's past.

The past reminds us. It does not define us.

Check out more from my colleague, Vala. His words of wisdom on Twitter stick with me. How about you? Here's a great reminder:

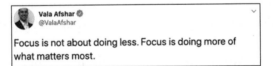

Vala Afshar
@ValaAfshar

Focus is not about doing less. Focus is doing more of what matters most.

You can find a new way forward. It just takes practice.

From 1986 to 1996, Notre Dame was a football powerhouse, led by the immortal and unforgettable Lou Holtz. When he heard about angry fans throwing oranges onto the field prior to Notre Dame's appearance in the Orange Bowl, Holtz told reporters, "I'm just glad we're not going to the Gator Bowl" (https://bit.ly/wfh-louholtz).

In 1986, Holtz hung a sign in the locker room, a sign that has since become legendary: "Play like a champion today." Before every home game, every Notre Dame player touches that sign before they take the field. In 1988, Notre Dame won a consensus national football title as Holtz posted a school record 23-game winning streak. His teams amassed an amazing 5-1 record in major bowls from 1988 to 1993.

Holtz knew the secret to playing like a champion: practicing like one first.

He always told his players, "Gentlemen, you practice like you play." In other words, the way you prepare for the game is the way you're going to play it. Today, that preparation is vital.

Any football coach will tell you that every play in their playbook is designed to score. That's right: they practice for their ultimate outcome, every time. Now, not every play results in a touchdown. We know that the opposing team is always a factor, people miss blocks, and sometimes there are fumbles on the play. Sometimes players get tackled for a loss. Sometimes it's three yards and a cloud of dust, or a quick first down. But you know what's always true? Winning teams prepare for success. And come what may, they are always playing the game. Playing to win. How about you?

Who said you couldn't set yourself up for success, every day? It's like the old saying goes, about thinking outside the box: "Who told you there was a box? And that there were rules?" Working from home is a time to expand your mindset and shift into new possibilities.

Maybe circumstances and market conditions are gonna jump up and oppose your best-laid plans. Sometimes life will punch you in the face, or knock you out of bounds. I know, I've been there.

Perhaps Marla in accounting is going to throw you for a loss. Penalties can happen in any game – even in the game of life. That's not a work from home thing, that's just the way the world works. But you can make sure you design your space and your calendar and your mindset to shift ... so that you give yourself an opportunity to make your world work for you.

Yes, my friend. Yes, you can design a place – a room of one's own – that serves you. Come what may, practice like you play. It's time to get in the game and play full out. Play to win.

The good news is: you've got home court advantage. You get to set up the game, the playing field, and the rules.

So many times, we think of success as something that's "out there." Away, in some far-off place, where it can never really be reached. But if you did the exercise, you just wrote down what success looks like. You made it personal. You defined the game of success on your own terms.

It's sort of like the decision to put stuff on your desk – like a paper clip, for example. Look at it. That tiny paper clip is a choice. Will it help you? If yes, keep it close by. If not, discard it and make room for something new.

Invest in a life design that serves you. Divest yourself of the things that do not. Play. To. Win.

How will you create a day that's satisfying, productive, and fulfilling? Shut the pantry from time to time. Be deliberate about your calendar. Set up your own guidelines for success, and you'll define it in your own terms. Got those rituals, routines, and boundaries set up? Good for you! Now it's time for the fun part: it's time to play the game.

HOME + WORK
Your Action Plan

- What's your routine for starting your day? How do you know you're not at work—what do you do, as a signal to yourself, that it's time to start or end the day?

- Mindfulness. Music. Movement. That's what I use to break up my day and clear my head. What works best for you?

- There's something you need to divest, right now. Something you need to let go of, so you can invest in something better. What is it?

- Think about the filters in your life. Do you need more, or less, or different ones?

- Write out your perfect day. Explore success. Expect it. What's that look like for you?

- When you design your office, you're defining the space where you will "play the game." What is it that would help you to enjoy your work, even more?

- What happens for you when you say, "Why not?"

Spectacular Online Meetings:
Your How-To Guide

I wanted to be in broadcasting.

When I was in college, I did these student broadcasts – little television shows for the university. I got to be a broadcaster on the public radio station. I covered the elections and even interviewed the governor. I loved it, even though it wasn't a career I decided to pursue.

Cut to the new normal. Now we're all in broadcasting. Don't believe me? Let's meet via Zoom and discuss.

It's time for an online meeting makeover. When it comes to video conferencing, there is a better way to broadcast – and to do that, we've got to take a look at where video calls fit into your home office.

Video calls are a great equalizer. It seems that everyone is equal in the virtual world. And we are all equally bad.

But you don't have to be.

If you're someone who loves to watch television shows and movies, now's the time to tune in to those experiences in a new way. Notice what's going on in the scene that's capturing your eye. What can you learn from the master storytellers in Hollywood (or, if it's Netflix, in Vancouver)? Could you incorporate what you see on HBO or Hulu into your next presentation? I'm not talking about wearing a costume, like Catherine the Great, or dropping in some Zoom background from outer space. I'm talking about noticing what captures your imagination. What about the YouTube stars you admire and follow? Beyond their topics, what's the style that captures your eye? Start binge watching with a purpose – because broadcasting and storytelling just became part of your job description.

What is it that's really engaging about a particular visual, whether it's a scene from a movie or a slide from a presentation? Notice what sparks your imagination and consider how you could bring that experience to bear in your next online meeting!

The problem, when it comes to virtual presentations, isn't that we *don't know* what to do. It's that we don't trust in ourselves to do it. What if you knew how to direct yourself, and your audience, so that your next presentation wasn't just clear and confident, it was fun?

Interaction is the key: creating and moderating a *conversation*, instead of just delivering a slide deck. The new model isn't a talking head on a news broadcast, per se. It's more like an interview. How can you create a dialogue in your next meeting – without it turning into a free-for-all?

Remember, time can blend together in a work-from-home world. In a video call, that twist of time can get people talking. That's especially true when it comes to asking people open-ended questions and then letting them go on-mic to share their inner monologue. Without the nonverbal cues and clues that are easily accessible in person, people may get lost in their own stories. It's an unintended consequence of the virtual meeting environment: some folks don't know when to stop talking. Do you?

> **Vala Afshar** ✓
> @ValaAfshar
>
> Excellence is not about next week, next month, or next job.
>
> Excellence is the next email.
> Excellence is the next meeting.
> Excellence is the next presentation.
> Excellence is the next phone call.

What can you do to drive feedback without letting your meeting or presentation get out of control? In preparation for my next book, *Listen Up!*, I gave a presentation to a group of people who lead customer experience (the book is all about how to listen to customers more effectively – an important aspect of customer experience and customer success). My prompt for everyone was: Who are the most unlikely allies you have found to help you in building your customer experience culture?

By asking this question, I did several key things:

1. **Prompt for What People Want and Need:** Everyone on the call was interested in finding allies and learning from other leaders what has been successful in different organizations. So I set the stage for some dialogue around something I knew the audience would value.

2. **Establish a Pattern:** By asking a question beforehand, I let people know that I was curious and interested in their insights and participation. And, after all, the book is called *Listen Up!*, so I decided to start with some listening (https://tinyurl.com/wfh-listenup). I carried that intention into the presentation. As a result, people came prepared to share their observations and to participate at a higher level.

3. **Small Moves, Big Impact:** Doing small things a little bit better than the other folks around you can make you really stand out. Don't underestimate the power of the chat window. What's one thing – one small thing – that you can do

to make yourself and your audience more comfortable? Got that idea in your head? Excellent – now, what's one more? Look in the direction of context: set the stage for your success, and make micro moves. You don't have to reinvent the virtual meeting model, just be a little better at the fundamentals than others. Small moves make a big difference in an online world.

Are you interested in standing out above the rest in your next virtual meeting? Here are some quick tips and strategies:

1. **Repeat the Good Stuff:** Consider what went right in your last presentation. What did you do that got the chat going, that got heads nodding, that got people thinking? What have you seen others do that you liked? How could you borrow from others to make their approach your own?

2. **Prepare a Prompt:** What's a compelling question that could start off your next presentation? If you want people to think and consider your ideas, give them an idea to consider!

3. **Quick Queries:** Can you send out one important idea-generating question prior to the virtual meeting? Getting people thinking is the objective here – you're not trying to use questions to diagram your remarks before you share them. Ask yourself: Will a well-thought-out agenda help people to explore new ideas, or will it help them to plan where they might want to check email in the middle of your keynote? Myself, I like to split the difference when sending out an agenda: I provide some important questions on what we're going to discuss, plus some solid real-time prompts that I save for the meeting. Even when I'm delivering a report or status update, I don't give the story away before I begin. Otherwise, why make it a presentation? Avoiding an overdetailed agenda is key. I accomplish two goals when I provide this powerful context: first, the folks who don't like

to be put on the spot can consider some responses before the meeting. Second, I'm also able to keep things fresh and spontaneous, so that no one can say "this meeting should have been an email." Consider carefully how much agenda you need to share and what info will help prompt the kinds of discoveries you hope for in your online conversation.

4. **Look Who's Talking:** Video presentations are best when interaction happens. What can you do to spark (and control) the kind of interaction you need? Think about the kinds of things you'd like to hear, either during or after you share your slides. Use this untapped skill as you create your next presentation: *curiosity*. What are you sincerely curious about? What do you need to know, right now – and can you come straight at that point? If there's not at least one question – one discovery – that needs to be made, you've got to wonder why you're having an online meeting in the first place.

5. **Moderation, That's the Moral:** If you give large webinars or presentations to groups, like I do, there's one key element you have to include in your next meeting: a moderator. Having someone moderate will help give you an extra set of eyes on the chat window – maybe even someone to help with your introduction, selecting people for live interaction, and more. My rule of thumb? Any meeting with a group of over eight people can benefit from moderation. Your number may vary, depending on your preference, audience, and topic – but eight is mine. For me, moderation is part of delivering an executive-level message, and keeping my focus (instead of getting distracted by every chat message or somebody turning off their video, for example). With a moderator, you're sharing another level of preparation and confidence. You don't have to go it alone!

What would happen if you started your preso (that's my little word for "presentation") like this:

You've seen the question I sent out to everyone. Here it is on the screen, once again. I've really simplified my slides, so that we can have a dialogue about the issues we all know are top of mind. We're all a little overwhelmed right now, so let me get right to the point: here are three key takeaways I want to discuss, and you can see them coming on screen now.

I don't want to spend the whole time looking at slides. I want to hear from you. So let me stop screen sharing and come back to the group. I'm going to begin with a poll, regarding our initiatives for our distributors in Canada [or whatever your key issue might be]. Let's start off with your feedback on this important challenge. Input your response whenever you are ready and we'll talk about the overall results as our first agenda topic.

Best Presentation Tips

What professional speakers do (that others do not) is *duplicate the consideration*, which is a fancy way of simply saying what people are thinking – verbalizing what's on everyone's mind. In the new normal, staying close to what people are thinking is the key to presentation success. Have the courage to say what you see. Say what you know to be true. Are you worried about being clever, funny, or impressive? Just be honest instead – it's a lot more compelling.

After all, we have this artificial environment – virtual video meetings – and that makes everyone thirsty for more authenticity, more compassion, and more consideration than ever before.

Recently, I chaired a global CIO council meeting. I was moderating a call where everyone was a tech titan, and the meeting took place on a new video platform. I came on early, got logged in, and was ready to go – but as people started joining, there was a glitch. For some reason, I was bumped off the call and everyone was struggling just to log in! Have you ever been there? There was a global audience and our virtual world was in turmoil. As you can imagine, my blood pressure went through the roof! I raced around trying to figure out what to do to help everyone. The one thing that kept me from calling the paramedics: we were all in the same boat. Turns out, a typo in the meeting password was the culprit. When we finally came together in our online meeting, it was with a spirit of *acknowledgment*. We all had a shared experience. My job as moderator was to *duplicate the consideration* – so I started off by mentioning how frustrated we all felt! By saying what people are feeling, you connect to the room in a way that helps people see your honesty and authenticity. "She gets it" is the nonverbal message that's sent, whether online or in person, to everyone on your video call.

Duplicating the consideration is a powerful skill, but you're already equipped to deliver it. You just have to say what people are thinking. Say the most honest thing you can. Have the courage to stop sharing your screen and instead share what's on everyone's mind.

You don't have to open a vein, tell people that they all need to lose weight, or confess your sins. But don't wait to get real in the virtual world. People are drawn to truth, now more than ever. Why not start there?

Don't hide behind your slides. Don't lean on your Power-Point as a script. Have your key points in the notes app on your phone, or on a piece of paper in front of you. That way, you've got your talking points without reading from the slides or letting the actual slides block you from really interacting with your audience. In every presentation, connection matters.

If you're nervous about your next presentation, I hear you. I'm right there, too. That's why I always build in an extra margin.

I plan for an extra 10 minutes to prepare and test the tech, especially when I'm presenting. When you take the stage virtually, technology is your scene partner. Just make sure that it doesn't play the villain in your next online performance.

But if it does, just remember that in a virtual world people are much more forgiving and understanding. If you're a senior leader and you're not, you're in for a surprise. Or a disappointment. Or both. Take a breath and be kind to yourself and others. Bring some consideration; sometimes tech tools don't cooperate.

If you've been on more than one video call, you know what I'm talking about! Deliver your next presentation from this understanding. Don't be afraid to laugh at yourself. But don't make a blooper reel your new script. There's no reason to make the same mistake twice, when you consider this fact: every online meeting is a learning opportunity. Your next presentation is a chance for you to step closer to success, even if you have to laugh at yourself along the way.

Video calls are a place for you to be creative in your message and your delivery. Sit down, stand up, experiment with your approach! Find what works best for you, and rehearse it. Practice success, so you play like a champion. Make up your mind to be authentic, provide prompts to spark a dialogue, and don't take yourself too seriously. That way, you'll learn from every call what's working and what's not.

Video calls start with great intentions but often end with unintended dissatisfaction. On the surface, you don't have to travel and no one else has to travel and you can make a personal face-to-face connection and everybody is on equal footing in their home offices and … well, what makes virtual presentations so tough? Maybe it's the fact that we're expecting Zoom to do it all. Do you default to video for every meeting and every conversation?

Nobody says, "Oh great! I get to do a Zoom call today!"

In the previous chapter, I shared three questions that can help you to tame your calendar. The first one was: *Does it have to be?* Now it's time to ask yourself: *Does it have to be onscreen?*

Whether you use Cisco Webex, Microsoft's Skype, Google Hangouts, or Facetime, the condition that we are all experiencing has become known as "Zoom fatigue."

The reason we get it wrong on video calls, in part, is because of the way we are wired.

Human beings learn to communicate around visual cues even more than verbal ones. From birth, we are attuned to nonverbal communication. An infant's movements synchronize to the speech of its caretaker from its first day of life, according to the *Wall Street Journal* (https://tinyurl.com/wfh-wsj1). We are conditioned for *synchrony* – a term that explains the coordination between environment, body language, and subtle clues that are often missed in a face-to-screen conversation. In video calls, it's nearly impossible to gather all the clues and cues we are used to from a face-to-face conversation. So people ramble. They check their phones, or email, or both. In a home office environment, distractions are many and visual cues are few.

"We've evolved to get meaning out of a flick of the eye. Our species has survived because we can produce [and quickly receive] those signals in a way that's meaningful," says Jeremy Bailenson, professor and director of Stanford University's Virtual Human Interaction Lab. "Zoom smothers you with cues, and they aren't synchronous. It takes a physiological toll."

What can you do in a virtual presentation to overcome this lack of synchrony, so that your ideas are heard, listened to, and understood? If you want to fight Zoom fatigue, consider that not every conversation needs to take place via video. Video is a useful tool, but don't overuse it. You don't always need to see everyone's background (or your own face staring back at you) when you connect with someone. Here's how you can be more selective before you go online:

Consider what action is needed for the issue you wish to discuss. Are you seeking greater personal connection with a diverse team, spread out across multiple countries? Or do you just need to get a quick review and approval on some budgetary numbers for next quarter? Choose the right tools for the job – especially when job #1 is communicating your ideas. It's easy to see that email, or texting, doesn't fit for every kind of interaction. That's also true for video calls. Consider the best way to share your message, remembering that falling back onto any one way of communicating is a limiting choice.

"Why are we having this presentation virtually?" Brant Pinvidic is saying, via a virtual video call. When he talks, he speaks as if he's on a roll – because he almost always is. You know the most high-energy person you've ever met? Brant runs laps around that guy.

He's standing up in his home office (which happens to be outdoors, to take advantage of the Southern California weather). He's wondering out loud why people aren't more deliberate about the way they approach virtual meetings.

Brant cares about how people show up online, with good reason. As a producer behind television shows like *Bar Rescue*, *Pawn Stars*, and *The Biggest Loser*, he's been involved in over 1,000 high-stakes pitch meetings. So far, he's sold over 300 TV and film projects to more than 40 different networks and distributors. A project that Brant conceived, produced, and directed, *Why I'm Not on Facebook*, received first prize at the Manhattan Film Festival. So far, his projects have grossed over $1 billion in revenues, earning Brant a reputation as the top pitchman in Hollywood. That reputation propelled his first book, *The 3-Minute Rule* (Portfolio/Penguin) to international best-seller status. So what advice can he give about how you can make a stellar debut in your next video call?

Brant says the secret to being virtually perfect on video starts with your priorities. "In *The 3-Minute Rule*, the whole idea is to cut out everything you *want* to say, and focus on what *needs* to be said," he shares.

"Competition is the core of business," Brant continues, his blond hair bouncing as he speaks. He's wearing a casual blue T-shirt and standing near a large center island with a built-in hibachi grill – part of an outdoor kitchen he's dubbed "Branti-hana."

The lanky outdoor chef and television producer says the key to online success is to prepare for it. "When you're out in the real world, people prep everything. They prep what they wear, they prep their opening remarks, they prep their slides, they work on their equipment." He steps out of the frame for a second. He's making sure his youngest son has prepped the veggies and shrimp (a little later, they'll be grilling something tasty at Brantihana). In a flash, he reappears on screen with more food for thought. "You don't go into a meeting with a major company to pitch your product – or into an investor meeting to pitch your idea – without understanding the elements around you. You wouldn't walk into an important conversation without being prepared." He stops to find his thought. "In a sense, to impress."

I wonder if that means you've got to put in some showman-ship, or razzle-dazzle of some kind. After all, some folks might not want to put *show business* into their work world. Brant replies without hesitation, "Who says all virtual presentations have to be boring?

"Hollywood show business actually has very little *show* to it," he says, echoing an emphasis on authenticity. "It's a very sensitive and mature marketplace where there is no room for gamesman-ship," he explains, referencing his work with biotech companies, politicians, entrepreneurs, and other businesses far from the studios in LA. Being prepared is good business, in any profession.

Don't wing it. Ever.

"If you had a Zoom presentation at two o'clock in the afternoon, and at one o'clock you started doing nothing but rehearsing it and getting it organized and considering the transitions between your slides, you're working in the right direction," Brant says. "That's one hour. That's 60 minutes of advantage, for you. Because I guarantee most people reading this right now have not been taking the time to prepare. They have a Zoom call at two o'clock and they show up at 1:59 and press the 'Join Meeting' button."

That's not preparation. That's not success. You're either showing that you don't understand the differences that exist in virtual presentations, or sending the message that you just don't care.

Leaders understand that just showing the same old slides isn't a process for adapting to the future of work. Bringing what's worked in the past into a brand-new environment is out of sync. And ineffective. Your slides and your delivery deserve a refresh. The new normal requires a readjustment so that your message isn't lost on yet another dull and uninteresting video call.

"What can you put into this presentation to show your audience that you've made an effort to make it exceptional for them?" Brant asks.

His voice rises, as he continues, "Why wouldn't you dedicate the same time and energy into your virtual presentation that you would have put into a physical, live presentation? In a face-to-face meeting, you would have driven there, maybe you got gas for your car, you paid for parking, spent time in traffic.... What if you invested that same amount of time into your next online presentation?"

Here's a quick checklist of things you can do to advance your career and your impact, just with a few simple changes:

1. **Upgrade Your Microphone and Camera:** In the previous chapter we talked about wearing headphones, and a headset is definitely a great place to start. But when it comes to creating clear audio, an external USB microphone is going to really up your game. If you want to stand out, add an external camera as well. You can go for 1080p or even 4K cameras that won't break your bank. Consider this to be a wise investment in your career, because better video and audio will help people to connect with you more easily. You'll be able to share the cues and clues that can make your communication stand out. (Want some ideas on the best tech for your home office? Check out Virtually Perfekt, for all things work-from-home related – including interviews and training from me. It's a great resource! [http://virtuallyperfekt.com].)

2. **Build Your Background:** You don't have to spend a lot of money to get a great-looking background. Maybe your company favors the green screen background that can be dropped in on Zoom or in other platforms. Maybe you invest in a simple curtain or a stand-up background. How about just placing some artwork on the wall behind you? Why not take the time to make sure you're standing in front of a backdrop that fits your career path and your intentions?

3. **Rethink Your Budget:** Brant asked me to imagine I was going on a customer-facing business trip. "What would you spend on that meeting?" he asks. "You might fly to the event. Stay overnight in a hotel. Rent a car or take a train to meet your client. What if you invested the cost of just one business trip into your virtual office setup?" As a producer, Brant's not afraid to invest in a good production. Are you? What would happen if you took the cost of a single business trip – just one trip! – and plowed it into your home office setup?

Simplify: Say Only What's Needed

It's counterintuitive, but fewer words can actually have more impact – especially when it comes to a presentation or pitch. Brant explains using a hypothetical: "Imagine you're getting married. You're going to have a big wedding. I've said that I can cater it for you. I come to you and I'm going to pitch you the idea of who I have as the chef for your event," he says, taking a pause to let me get a clear picture in my mind. "How do I do that?" he asks, rhetorically.

"My pitch has four words: *I've got Gordon Ramsey*," he says.

I'd say that pretty much covers it.

Why are your PowerPoint slides so complicated? Can you see that simple is stronger? Simple and honest and jam-packed with value means that your message is impossible to ignore. The pros don't use a bazillion words, flowery language, and unbearably dense slides. It's not show business, it's smart business: true leaders tell you the one thing you need to know.

Brant advises a three-step approach to making better online presentations – he calls his method the Triple D. In order to nail the online presentation, you have to:

1. Have a *Directive*
2. Be *Direct*
3. Be the *Director*

Having a directive means that you know what you want to get out of this meeting. You are clear on why the meeting exists and why you are having it via Zoom. There needs to be a compelling reason why people are seeing your screen, instead of just receiving a PDF via email. Do you need to be able to walk people through a pitch deck or complex document so that you can guide them toward the highlights and key issues? Do you need to gather feedback in real time as your story unfolds?

If you want to be directive, cover less content and provide way more context. Advance agendas and the role of attendees are critical. Meeting notes and next-steps documentation are a necessity, not an option. Virtual meetings are even more prone to misunderstandings, so get crystal-clear on why this meeting is a video call, who you need in the (virtual) room, and what roles you need people to assume. Look in the direction of success. That way, you'll recognize it when it shows up – you won't be taken completely by surprise. As Brant says in *Forbes*, don't just plan for success. Prepare for it (https://bit.ly/wfh-pinvidic).

Being direct means coming straight to the point, with an economy of words. People get long-winded on Zoom; audiences get distracted. Do everyone a favor, and cut out the fluff. If you can make your 30-minute presentation fit into a 20-minute slot, *do it*. Who says that a meeting has to be 60 minutes, anyway? The entire world has changed, so why are we still trying to fit our online meetings into yesterday's time containers? Because that's what we're used to? The new normal is *new*. Are you using yesterday's solutions to find tomorrow's results? The Great Pause is a great time to reflect and redirect your message and your resources.

As an author, I've discovered that good writing is rewriting. Have you chosen the words and the slides that can help you most? It's time to trim the extra slides. Hire a coach or work with a mentor to help you to choose your words more carefully. Don't go online until you've had someone review what you've created, if you really want to make sure you're making an impact. (Virtually Perfekt has tons of resources, including presentation coaching and guidance. You might even catch a glimpse of Brantihana there as well [http://virtuallyperfekt.com].)

Finally, in the midst of too much information and too many distractions, people want to be directed. In order for a virtual presentation to work effectively, it's up to you to drive the story by telling people what's important. Your job is to guide people exactly where to look. "When you watch a film or TV show," Brant says, stepping into the director role, "it's never done with a single, static camera the entire time." The director guides each shot, taking time to consider what's most important. How can you help your audience to focus on what matters? Where do you want your audience to look, listen, and learn?

When Brant delivers a pitch, he puts power into his PowerPoint. He does it in his studio – with three cameras, a video switcher, and a microphone so fantastic that it makes it sound like his speech is coming from inside your own head. (Check out his website to get a feel for what I'm talking about at http://brantpinvidic.com.) But, to be clear, you don't need three cameras to execute the Triple D strategy. You just need to think about how you can create and introduce some variety into your work.

Virtual meetings don't have to be boring, nerve-wracking, or dull. And you don't have to be a television producer to create good content – but it helps if you learn from one. Give your slide deck a haircut, pronto. Stop sharing your screen and share what's really on your mind. Set clear directives and expectations.

You've seen how to use virtual meetings to broadcast your best message – a message that's interactive and guided, well-rehearsed and deliberate. Video calls don't have to be your go-to, but even if you use GoToMeeting, you'll still be ready with greater preparation than ever before. Upgrade your context and your prep work beyond what others are doing – don't just wing it. Consider how you can shape the discoveries people need to make via virtual meetings. That way, you're directing your next online presentation toward success. And you'll be the star of the show.

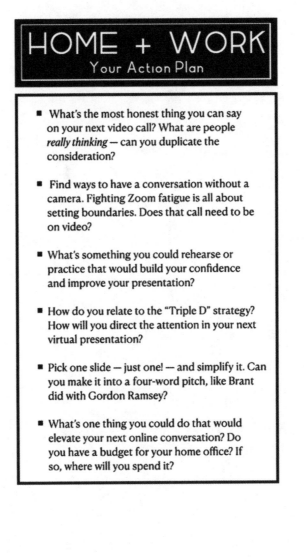

HOME + WORK
Your Action Plan

- What's the most honest thing you can say on your next video call? What are people *really thinking* — can you duplicate the consideration?

- Find ways to have a conversation without a camera. Fighting Zoom fatigue is all about setting boundaries. Does that call need to be on video?

- What's something you could rehearse or practice that would build your confidence and improve your presentation?

- How do you relate to the "Triple D" strategy? How will you direct the attention in your next virtual presentation?

- Pick one slide — just one! — and simplify it. Can you make it into a four-word pitch, like Brant did with Gordon Ramsey?

- What's one thing you could do that would elevate your next online conversation? Do you have a budget for your home office? If so, where will you spend it?

Team Building, Collaboration, and Leading Remote Teams

"That green elf was a liar," Hanna explains.

She's part of a team that just solved the mystery of the Grimm Escape. Do you know what that is? According to *Fast Company*, and Hanna, it's not a video game. It's an online version of an escape room, from Seattle-based game maker Puzzle Break (https://bit.ly/wfh-escaperoom).

In case you're not familiar, an escape room is a game where a team of players assemble and agree to be locked in a room together. The objective is simple: to escape. Typically, the space is a themed chamber that's full of oddities and curiosities: mysteries needing to be solved. The players have to cooperate to discover clues, solve puzzles, and accomplish tasks in a specific amount of time, so that they can (wait for it) escape the room. However, with the arrival of the coronavirus, most live escape rooms were placed on permanent lockdown.

Luckily for Puzzle Break co-founder and CEO Nate Martin, online escape rooms are open for business. Companies found out that remote workers can still get in a game together. Players don't have to physically be in the same room in order to participate. The online escape room, he says, is a great team-building tool. Hanna nods her head in agreement.

"You interact online with 'fairy godparents,'" she explains, with a straight face. Puzzle Break staff members – aka fairy godparents – serve as guides to the groups, offering answers to players and providing hints to the perplexed. So what does the Grimm Escape have to do with team building, collaboration, and leading remote teams?

Everything.

Exploring new worlds and new environments in a collaborative online game is a metaphor for our times. True, the escape room scenario helps remote workers escape boredom, but there's more to it than that. The problem-solving skills are  a super-relevant simulation, helping people to find new ways to collaborate around this question: How do we get out of our current situation? Isn't that the question for our times, right now?

Nate Martin explained the appeal of his online world to Mashable: "In our physical rooms, for some teams, it's every person for themselves. In the virtual space, time and time again – and we didn't predict this – we are seeing united groups" (https://bit.ly/wfh-escaperoom1). Companies are using online escape rooms to help people connect, engage, and collaborate in a fantasy environment, because it drives skills for the real one.

Companies like UK-based ClueQuest also offer online escape rooms, work-from-home kits, and more (https://bit.ly/wfh -cluequest). If you still think you can't collaborate and perform team-building activities for a remote workforce, Hanna and her fairy godparents would disagree.

More business-focused solutions for collaboration are coming online every day, providing high-powered virtual whiteboards, project maps, and more for important processes. Companies like Cisco, Netflix, and Twitter are turning to powerful apps like Miro (http://miro.com) for online collaboration. Designed around distributed teams, this online platform is more than just a shared space: it's an online whiteboard for mapping, diagramming, and delivering the collective brainstorm of your team. Need to do a design sprint? Want to know what online environments have worked best for others, from product design to manufacturing blueprints to UX (user experience) flow? Check out the "Miroverse" – a growing online depository of awesome customer experiences, affinity diagrams, and more. There are a myriad of other tools out there, including Slack, Mural, Hive, Microsoft Whiteboard... the list goes on and on (http://slack.com, http://mural.co, http://hive.com, https://bit .ly/wfh-whiteboard).

What's going to be the right platform for you and your organization? Of course, the answer depends on your needs: Are you looking for help with project management, onboarding, software design, research and development? A quick search will reveal what's available in a more up-to-date format than this one. However, the specifics aren't the point of the story. Availability is.

Andrew's Story

How does a guy from Indiana get invited to meet the Queen of England? Well, ask Andrew Lannerd: because he's gone to her birthday party. Twice.

Andrew is an anglophile: he loves all things from the UK, most especially the Royal Family. How far would you be willing to go, for the thing you love? For Andrew, he moved 3,987 miles from the Midwest to London, bringing with him a lifetime collection of spectacular English memorabilia. I know because I helped him set up his home (or is it a museum?) in the UK.

Andrew runs Transcendent Travel, a company specializing in a behind-the-scenes look at the things that make the UK unique, special, and regal. Guess how his travel business is doing in a coronavirus economy? Yeah, you guessed right.

Lannerd has reinvented. Tours aren't happening, but memorabilia is big business. Turns out, the Queen's menu from a Christmas Day luncheon is a coveted keepsake—one of many he's cultivated over the years, following the Royal Family from Balmoral to Buckingham Palace.

Instead of bringing tour groups to Britain, he's discovered new ways of connecting clients to the UK. Working from home means reinvention; Lannerd has turned his passion for British culture into a curated experience online.

What can you use to repurpose and reinvent, offering your expertise in new ways to new clients?

Smart companies are seeing that you can sustain productivity, collaboration, and employee engagement even when managing a remote workforce. You just have to reconsider how your processes and tools need to shift in a work-from-home world. And adaptability is key to success.

That's according to Patty Hatter, Senior Vice President for Global Customer Services at Palo Alto Networks. The early morning sunlight streams through her California home office window and reflects intermittently off her black-framed glasses. Balancing a stoneware coffee mug in her right hand, she recalls team dynamics in a pre-COVID world.

"I'll never forget having to close our offices in a single afternoon," she says, and pauses. Palo Alto's value proposition is based, in part, on having customer support teams on customer sites all over the world. When the coronavirus hit, the very fabric of their business changed. How could they deliver solutions when their employees weren't on-site anymore?

"There were employees walking to their cars juggling office equipment and a rising sense of panic while still talking to our customers on the phone. Meanwhile, we were trying to locate all of our employees who were out on customer sites," Patty shares. Day 1 was chaotic, for the company's 7,000 employees – and their customers. What was this new normal, and how long would it last?

As offices were emptying, customer support calls were spiking. Palo Alto Networks provides software and hardware products to help companies keep their information – and their workforce – safe. And when every organization in the world goes virtual at the same time, information security is as critical as employee safety.

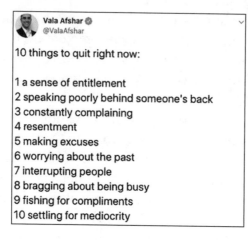

"New product support calls increased 400% when we went into lockdown," Patty shares. "Our overall contact volume went up 200% and has stayed at that level since those early days."

Patty was concerned. She considered the toll the increased workload might take, when combined with juggling family commitments, home office concerns, and all of the things we've talked about so far. Would a spike in volume mean a spike in burnout? Would her team be able to respond to increased demand in a work-from-home world?

"People could just work themselves into the ground," she says, shaking her head. "Overwork is not sustainable. Especially when you consider what people are dealing with personally during this time as well."

I've known Patty for nearly 20 years. Once again I see the compassion in her face as she talks about how much she cares about her team. She is one of the most empathetic communicators I have ever encountered in my career. I'm imagining what it must have been like for her, balancing massive business transformation along with an unprecedented spike in activity.

"We encouraged people to take time off," Patty says, reflecting on the dedication of her team. "But people felt hesitant to step away."

That's when Patty turned to the most effective tool any leader can deploy: *listening*.

She and her leadership team asked for feedback. They compared what they heard with an employee engagement survey from earlier in the year. One theme was consistent: *help us bring our full selves to work*. What would that look like inside of the current changes? Patty went to work on a holistic approach to working from home.

"We had a culture where people didn't have to have their video on," Patty says, reflecting on pre-COVID conference call behavior. "Now, we've realized that not using your camera impedes connection and collaboration. People get called out if we can't see someone! There's a craving for connection and our culture has shifted towards greater collaboration. Everyone is turning their camera on now. Plus I've never seen the chat feature used so much." Connection and visibility were small steps she implemented wherever and whenever she could. And she wanted a forum for real-time feedback - as well as a chance for people to connect around the virtual water-cooler.

One night a week, she holds an informal meeting at 8 p.m. for all of her direct reports. There's joking and crosstalk, of course, but the idea is to create a space for connection. The conversation centers on family, hobbies, memories, and friendships. Do you talk about work? "Yes," she shares, "but it's more of a time for people just to decompress."

During office hours, there was another shift: Zoom meeting protocol was set aside to account for personal lives. Attending to the matters of the moment took precedence, and leaders adapted and adjusted accordingly. Interacting with kids was welcomed, as long as folks could do so while still focusing on work issues.

The shifts resulted in unexpected innovation. "One of our employees in Tel Aviv offered a class for parents and children: *An Introduction to Cybersecurity for Kids*," Patty shares proudly. "The program enabled kids to see what their parents were working on," she says. Inviting kids into the world of work (even in a small way) went a long way in elevating the company's engagement.

Ultimately, listening paid off, Patty says. "We had an increase in our customer satisfaction, even with the giant spike in activity." Innovation around employees created better service for their customers, not worse. "It's remarkable, and almost unheard of in the services world," she says, reflecting on what the company gained in the transition to a work-from-home workforce.

Want to empower even greater collaboration from remote teams? Compress your timeline for meetings.

"Number one, you just can't do a three-hour working session anymore," Kevin Collins explains from his office in the East Bay, near San Francisco. He's the Managing Director of Software and Platforms Industry at Accenture, a consulting company with over half a million employees worldwide.

An adorable blonde-haired child pops her head into the frame. In an instant she's grabbed Kevin, her arms wrapped around his neck. She's wearing a full-length pink nightgown with white stars. Pushing her face into his ear she says, full voice, "How's your conference call, Daddy?" Kevin pulls back and erupts into laughter, and so do I. I'm guessing this isn't the first time that Violet has pulled this stunt. From this angle, I can see she's got a huge stuffed green frog wedged into the hug. I think the frog's name is Filbert, but I'm not sure – she told me once but I forgot. Whatever his name is, he's smashed into Kevin's neck, his googly eyes popping up over Violet's shoulder. Kevin loves it – in a swift move he cradles his daughter and the unnamed frog in his lap. "The call," he says to his captive listener, bending over to pull closer until his nose is within millimeters of hers, "is going GREAT!" He tickles her into more laughter. Maybe it's my fault for calling him after hours, but it seems like a happy accident. She escapes his hug and waves to me. "Bye, Karen!" she says, as she drags her frog back to the hidden corners of their house.

Regaining his composure, but not losing his smile, Kevin continues, "Three-hour working sessions are dead," referencing the bread and butter of most consultants. Here's how Accenture is battling distraction, compressing time, and rethinking teamwork in the new normal:

1. **Turn Up Your Text Messages:** "It was an important proposal for a client. I had sent a few emails," Kevin begins. "No response. I wasn't worried I was being ghosted, I just knew my contact was busy. So I recorded a less-than-one-minute video message, as I was walking Matti," he says, referencing his 105-pound Bernese Mountain Dog. In the video, with his canine co-star, he shared three quick takeaways from his last client conversation. A neighbor walked by while Kevin was filming the video. Kevin said hi, finished his points in less than a minute, and sent the video via text to his client. His phone rang 15 minutes later: it was his client. He wanted to talk about Matti and how Kevin said hello to his neighbor. The human element begins a business conversation, Kevin points out. He's not afraid to keep it real: whether it's hugging his kids or walking his dog, he never ignores what walks into the video frame.

Because, with Kevin, what you see is what you get. "I am getting faster and better responses on short video messages than I have ever gotten on texts. If there's a way to send something unexpected and non-work-related in your message, it really helps. People are quick to call me back to talk about how Matti tried to eat a plant

This is Matti.

during my last Zoom call, for example." That human element is where the boundaries come down and the connection begins. But be careful, he warns: text videos are only for people you know; he doesn't advise using them for prospecting, only follow-ups. When I follow up to tell him I'm going to open his story with Violet giving him a big hug, he smiles and says, "I like your style."

2. **Compress Your Timeline:** Kevin and his teams would often deliver three-hour meetings, or even a 1½-day strategy session, for clients. Today, that approach is obsolete. Those customer strategy sessions have been broken down into a series of five 90-minute meetings, over the course of a week. And he's still looking for ways to compress time everywhere, using more meetings and shorter time frames to drive results. The only way to hold people's attention? Don't press your limits. Or theirs.

3. **Deconstruct the Demo:** Do you deliver demos in your presentations? For Accenture, that's an everyday practice. But Kevin says it doesn't have to be a live demo. "We've discovered how to mix the live demo with some prerecorded pieces. Because trying to balance the presentation with the tech with watching the chat and the client – there are a lot of moving parts. If we try to do everything live, something can break." You don't have to do or demonstrate everything, if you're showing something that's existing technology and not a big leap. If everyone on the call can see how something can be done, that's a lot more positive than having to apologize for an overengineered demo that flops on your client call.

4. **Tighten Up Your Choreography:** In Kevin's world, multiple parties are required to prepare and deliver on their consulting engagements – complex arrangements that can take hours or days just to explain. For his high-stakes business meetings, a team of experts could be interfacing

with 30 or more team members on the customer side. Preparing for the client interaction – the one that has been divided into segments, never more than 90 minutes in length – has changed to address the complexities that can arise online. Now, team members participate in 15-minute check-in meetings as part of the customer choreography. As ideas are developed – the choreography that Kevin is talking about – his team members know they must meet with everyone involved. The idea is that everyone on the team must be able to articulate the entire customer strategy, while certain subject matter experts dive deeper into their areas of expertise.

5. **Manage Micro Meetings:** These 15-minute micro-meetings deliberately build collaboration into the process. Who can say no to a 15-minute meeting? "In our world, no one. People are much more willing to weigh in, especially when you don't have to jump on a plane and fly to New York or Nashville to get an answer." Accenture's collaborative model is based on gaining a yes more frequently than ever before. Kevin continues, "We're crowdsourcing our projects, internally. We're being deliberate about saying, 'Here's what we're thinking. Here's how we think this impacts you. What do you think?' We're having the ability to get much bigger teams engaged and it's flattened out our organization and increased buy-in. And the process really helps our clients. It helps our chances of getting a project, and we feel like we are putting out a better work product." How could your company incorporate micro-meetings before you deliver your next message? If a successful meeting is really just a series of positive responses, what are you doing to drive that culture of collaboration within your own team?

6. **Unfinish Your Slides:** "We used to come into a presentation with finished slides, right? Because that's what a virtual presentation is: we're *presenting* over here." It's counterintuitive, but Kevin says a finalized approach means you're finished before you start. "Finished slides are a lot less personal, a lot less interactive, a lot less about the client and more about what we've thought up. That's not co-creation." So what's the unfinished answer? Kevin says the team will provide a straw man slide – talking points around what they believe to be the top-of-mind issues for the client. They appoint a presentation scribe – someone who doesn't participate in the customer presentation, per se. The scribe's job is to collect what's said around a particular issue and format all viewpoints into a new and updated slide. The team moves on to another issue while the scribe creates the revisions. About 10 minutes later, the updated slide is created – co-created – and shared with the client. When the scribe signals that the new product is ready, everyone on the call sees evidence of the collaboration. "And then we can go to the next iteration," Kevin concludes. How could you use a dedicated scribe to capture what's said in a collaborative meeting? Are your slides ever really final until the client weighs in? What would happen to your culture if you decided that a slide wasn't finished until the client saw it and shared their thoughts on it? What if you provided your presentation as a starting point for dialogue, and then you finished your client presentation as a cohesive, collaborative team?

7. **Let's Vote On It:** "We've doubled down on using polls and quizzes," Kevin says. Asking people to raise their hands is a quick way to overcome the hesitancy around commenting on camera, especially in groups where people don't know each other. When participants are from diverse organizations, or even the same one, polls and check-ins are a great

way to get some interaction. When you want to get feed-back, build collaboration into the process. And put it up for a vote.

8. **Segment Your Sections:** In live meetings, cues and clues were easily visible in the meeting room. You could tell when people were understanding and agreeing much more easily. Online, without complete synchrony, you have to build in breaks to confirm your progress. "In a 45- or 60-minute session, we'll build in four or five stops. We'll restate what we've heard and shared, and give people a chance to raise a hand or to object to an idea. Or to say, 'well, I saw that differently.'" It's tempting to fall into a trap of your own assumptions and context. That's why a planned pattern interrupt can be so valuable: don't assume that silence means agreement in an online call. Even stepping away for a minute can give participants a moment for a new thought, comment, or realization. The built-in break strategy is all about buy-in: leaving nothing to chance or misinterpretation. Are these periodic check-ins working? "Karen, it's one of the things I wish we had been doing all along," Kevin confesses.

9. **Prepare for Success:** I shared with Kevin that I've seen a lot of folks coming into meetings without preparation – with little or no adjustment for the new normal. Kevin has a different viewpoint: "Because of the risks of stepping over each other, missing visual cues and other challenges with online presentations, we're rehearsing more, not less. A greatly needed skill in our context is to do the upfront work." Have you ever witnessed a webinar where six people are presenting and the handoffs are a confused mess? I have, and it's deadly. For Accenture, coordination has to be built into their choreography. "For our last 90-minute session, we spent about six or seven hours, in total, designing everything from our approach to who would carry what

part of the story." Kevin is more orchestrated, not less, in a virtual meeting, advocating a 4:1 model (four hours of prep for one hour of delivery) for presentations. "When you've got analytics work, marketing work, business strategy work, finance, numbers … it's all under the guidance of the leadership team but people are working independently. When we get to within a couple of weeks of the client meeting, we come together to draw out the big picture. In this virtual world, we're expected to be very explicit about stitching together the component parts of our recommendations, from technology to operations and everything in between. Every team member needs to be able to deliver the basics of the whole story. And that takes a new level of coordination and preparation." I think I need to introduce him to Brant Pinvidic; it seems these two guys have a lot in common.

10. **Make Room for Improvisation:** "I bet it sounds like the increased level of preparation removes all of the improvisation from the client engagement," Collins says, reflecting on the structure he's put in place. "What I'm finding is just the opposite." It's the diligence and attention to detail that allows the team to be free to create and improvise in front of the client. Like an actor practicing a part, the artistry comes after you've got all your lines down pat. I can tell you from experience: you have to know your role inside and out - it's that diligence that provides the path to freedom and creativity. "Because we're all aligned on messaging and understand the research, analysis, and technology, we are more improvisational in the actual session - not less. I know that's counterintuitive, but it's sort of like the old saying about how you have to understand the box in order to think out of it." Ultimately, there is an opportunity for greater freedom, not less, through preparation.

11. **Every Conversation Is About Change:** Consulting companies are asked to make recommendations and weigh in on company strategy on a regular basis. As Kevin says, "Our clients are expecting us to do more around change management than ever before. They want to know how to get their organization aligned around these new initiatives – so we're being asked to help them to get buy-in within every part of the organization." The emphasis on guidance and service and change management isn't exclusive to consulting. In the new normal, every conversation for every customer is about change. How are you looking past your products and services to see how you can help companies with the challenges of our time: adoption, adaptation, and implementation? What are you doing to help lead others through change? The world is starving for solutions around change. Why not start there? The future belongs to companies that not only adopt a culture of collaboration, but that know how to share that same spirit with their clientele.

Recently, I participated in a fireside chat with Harish Dwarkanhalli, President of Wipro Limited (a division of one of the largest IT consulting companies in India). The moderator was Gurvinder Singh Sahni, Chief Marketing Officer of Appirio, a Wipro company. I was quietly amazed at Gurvinder's expert moderation – it made the meeting come to life. Our conversation was fast-paced, informative, clear, and (dare I say it?) really fun. The reason our dialogue was so energizing for all of us on the call? Gurvinder's commitment to preparation.

Gurvinder did a masterful job of research upfront about each guest, myself included. As a result, he was able to be very thoughtful about the questions he was going to ask. He cared about what we were going to discuss. He didn't just Google my name; he did a prep call with me and made sure to ask if I was okay with him sharing certain things. In fact, he came up with some pretty obscure (but really relevant) stuff!

On the call, he was a steadfast moderator, but not in an oppressive way. So I'm one of three guests: one in India, one in New Jersey, the other guy in Boston. We're laughing and interacting like old friends, thanks to Gurvinder. It was energizing.

The conversation was engaging, not just for the panelists but for every attendee. Because someone (our moderator) was orchestrating the magic, based on the work he had done in advance. His attention to detail allowed everyone on the panel to show up at their best. Additionally, his preparation brought a natural chemistry to the call.

That consideration – that attention to detail and preparation – is what's needed in every virtual meeting. Who's your emcee? Who's your moderator? Have you done your homework and put in the legwork so that everyone is at ease?

When you consider how you conduct your virtual meetings, whether you're leading a team or connecting with customers halfway around the globe, invest in the kind of preparation that will help take your interaction to the next level. You don't have to sacrifice chemistry or conversation, if you look at collaboration in new ways. And in an upcoming chapter, we explore how companies are replacing live events with online meetings with surprising results. Believe it or not, the new normal is allowing the virtual workforce to be more engaged (and productive) than ever before. But first: let's talk about some family matters – and how to corral the kids.

- If every persuasive conversation is about change, what's the change you propose? And what's the impact of that change?

- How will you (and perhaps your team) rehearse for your next presentation? What's the pre-work that's going to make you more confident and effective?

- When you give a presentation, how do you encourage folks to use the chat window – and are you using polls and quizzes?

- Think about the questions you can ask, prior to your next meeting, pitch, or sales presentation. What's going to be the prompt that serves you best?

- Would you have the courage to leave your slides a little "raw" for your next client conversation – and ask them to help you fill in the details and polish, so that you truly collaborate?

6

How to Corral the Kids

"I'm not a rocket scientist. But I work with a few of them," Patricia Moore explains from her home office. She lives just a few miles away from the Johnson Space Center, south of Houston. The mother of two is sitting next to her husband, Jack, at the kitchen table. We're on a Zoom call, chatting about her youngest daughter, Evelyn, who can be, well, kinda demanding. How demanding is kinda demanding? I ask.

"We call her 'the Honey Badger,'" Patricia shares, explaining that the Honey Badger takes what she wants and doesn't take no for an answer. The name comes from when she was a toddler: They would tell her "no" and she would just go on and do whatever she wanted, as if her parents weren't even there.

An adorable little girl with a twinkle in her eye and a pixie haircut comes into frame. Evelyn is nine years old, wearing a swimsuit and carrying a towel draped over her left arm.

She doesn't look like a honey badger to me. What kind of unreasonable demands will this sweet child in a beach outfit bring to our conversation?

She marches over to Patricia, who leans down to hear her whisper an important question into her ear. Patricia turns to her and explains that they will be leaving in just a few minutes. Evelyn smiles at her dad and leaves as quickly as she entered. Their exchange was so polite! Was that the Honey Badger, or Miss Manners?

Sometimes it's easy to feel like juggling homeschooling and work from home can be a no-win scenario: you're always doing something poorly. But Patricia and Jack have figured out a routine that has created a surprising amount of maturity, responsibility, and personal growth for their two adorable girls. Plus, the couple confirms that their professional productivity has never been higher. Turns out, you can juggle two careers, homeschooling, and one honey badger. But it wasn't always easy.

Patricia is a communications specialist, focused on museum outreach for the Johnson Space Center, the crown jewel in America's space program. Prior to the coronavirus travel restrictions, she traveled the country helping students to understand how NASA's human space exploration is changing our world. She regularly works with museums, providing presentations that leverage her background in elementary education in addition to her work as a spokesperson for the Space Center.

The tall guy with the cool sideburns is her husband, Jack. He's the exhibits manager for NASA's Johnson Space Center. He coordinates with scientists and engineers on NASA's technical accomplishments, translating that work into museum exhibits that explain the unique stories from the Johnson Space Center. Pre-COVID, a big part of his work was focused on fabrication – visiting sites and holding in-person meetings to make sure designs are coming to life.

Now, everything in their world has changed – from the nature of their jobs to the way they educate their kids. What's a family to do when travel is shut down, fabrication plants aren't taking visitors, and the Honey Badger is full of surprises?

Jack begins, "You know, it's interesting 'cause with Tricia's job, she's kind of already working from home. She did two days a week working from home and she'd go in to do some of the virtual events. And so it was a little bit more of a natural transition for her. For me, I was really in an area where it was very uncomfortable, because being at home is not my realm. I'm very much 'boots on the ground': I used to spend maybe two hours in the office and the rest of my time running around, meeting with clients, doing site visits, going over to check on jobs. And I've had to figure out how to do all that virtually." Patricia talks about how all of her work has shifted online – and her employer has invested in a home studio setup, so she can broadcast her message without getting on a plane. But what about the Honey Badger?

"We went through some difficult phases, when we first tackled the home school stuff," Jack explains, sharing that their oldest daughter, Elizabeth, just turned 12. Jack holds up a picture so I can see her beautiful long hair and coy smile.

I ask whether Patricia's background as an educator helped her to corral her kids and make learning from home more effective.

Patricia laughs for a full 45 seconds straight, begins to weep, and nearly falls out of her chair.

Jack says, "When we first moved into learning from home, we entered phase 1: grinding our gears." The schoolteachers hadn't figured out what a manageable workload looked like, so they basically threw the book at their students' parents and expected them to sort it out. "There was so much to do," Patricia says, "and it instantly became a time management

A honey badger?

ment exercise. At first, the girls would come in every 15 to 20 minutes to talk to me, and it was breaking up what I was doing." You can hear the frustration in her voice as she brings back the memory. "Now we have a routine where we say, 'you can talk to Momma and Daddy at these times and until then it's up to you to get as much figured out on your own as you can.'"

Seems like that's what we're all trying to do: figure things out and schedule times for interaction and feedback. Notice how rituals, routines, and boundaries once again show up as the keys to success.

The Moores would begin their workday while the kiddos were asleep, then get the girls going on their assignments. Surprisingly, what worked best for the parents is the exact strategy that works in a company: providing guidance, expecting greater ownership on assignments, and measuring the results.

Their girls became incredibly resourceful and self-monitoring – surprising both of their parents. Have we been underestimating ourselves – and our kids – all this time?

"We told them, here's the work you need to do," Jack says, "and if you get done by Thursday, you get a three-day weekend. You just have to get it done." The couple set up clear boundaries about when they would and wouldn't be available for guidance and questions. They carved out office space for everyone: Jack already had the front office, and Patricia reconfigured her own space near the dining room – plus they transformed a guest bedroom into her studio. The girls had their very own homework table that Jack built for them.

"Phase 2, we got settled into a rhythm," Patricia says, as she elaborates on a recent school assignment: the Honey Badger was learning how to email. The teacher would send over an assignment to Patricia, who would forward the email to her daughter. She had to open the attachment (part of the assignment) and read the instructions in the pdf. Evelyn would go over the info by herself, click the links, and reply to her mom via email (that was the assignment, after all). Her older sister, Elizabeth, also started doing things a lot more independently.

They did it for the same reasons you and I work: ultimately, they wanted to get out and play. The girls did what they needed to do so that they could do what they wanted to do. That doesn't sound like child's play to me. That sounds like a valuable life lesson for all of us.

Turns out that we're all capable of more than we thought possible. That's true for kids, parents . . . and companies. "Her big sister, Elizabeth, wanted to work on the couch wrapped in a blanket with the dog in her lap," Jack says, frowning. "I wanted her to work from the table we had set up. But you pick your battles, right? I told her she could do her work from the couch but only if she got a 90 or higher on her assignment." When she turned in a 100 in record time, Jack rethought the idea of micromanagement. And realized perhaps that Elizabeth is a skilled negotiator. Maybe being comfortable is part of being smart? That's true for kids, just like it is for adults.

Of course, there was the time when the Honey Badger did her math homework in record time, got a 100, and didn't show any of her work. Patricia says, "She told me, 'Momma, I'm done!' and I said, 'How are you done with that worksheet so fast and you didn't have to show any work?'" Turns out the teacher had accidentally attached the answer key to the homework assignment. Patricia missed it, but the Honey Badger grabbed it and did not want to let it go.

"Now we're in phase 3, which is kinda magical, where the kids understand the mechanics of everything. They know it's their job to find their assignments, they know when they need to be working, and when we are available," Jack continues. "We provide guidance and give them the chance to work at their own pace," Patricia chimes in. Jack says, "Then we can put more focus on getting our stuff done." He goes on to say that working from home is actually much better than being in an office.

"In an office, people would stop by and check in with me all during the day, which is great – except it's not," he explains, because of the way he works. He'll often be on complex projects where breaking his train of thought causes him to retrace his steps. He likes to methodically focus on a single process. Jack says he'd never realized it, but minor interruptions were causing major delays. As a result of working from home, and managing interruptions much more effectively, his productivity has gone through the roof. Video calls and handheld factory tours have given him the assurances he needs to manage his projects.

"My boss made it very clear: I expect you to be working and available until 5 p.m. Then your time is your own," Jack says, echoing that boundaries start at the top. And if he needs greater flexibility, to help with homework assignments or whatever the case may be, options are readily available. "The key is to communicate what you need," he says. "And if you have to work while the kids are sleeping or after they go to bed, that's just what you do," he continues, echoing the feelings of parents all over the world. "I'd coordinate with Tricia when she had a big meeting during the day, to make sure I was on deck and available at that time. And I had to let the girls know that they don't always have to go to their mom, which was their default at first. It's all about how you communicate," he finishes.

Meanwhile, Patricia says she doesn't have to be at NASA at all to do her job. "The only thing I can't do is live site visits," she says, elaborating on how her home studio has made video meetings easier than ever. But what's most surprising about working from home full time? She has never had more energy.

> "Piglet noticed that even though he had a Very Small Heart, it could hold a rather large amount of Gratitude."
> -A. A. Milne, Winnie the Pooh

"I never realized what a drain it was to get the girls ready for school, head in to work, deal with everything, and all the running around. Don't get me wrong, I love my job and I don't have a 45-minute commute or anything like that. I love to travel, too – but without those additional obligations . . ." Her voice trails off as she stops to take a breath. Then she says, almost in a half-sigh, a single word: "Wow." She realizes that the good ol' days weren't all that good. And in the new normal, she's feeling like a new woman. Her kids are thriving, and her husband is smiling (and sharing in the responsibilities so that they both can thrive). Patricia says she's never going back to the way things were before. Jack nods in agreement.

The changes that have been thrust upon us can be liberating, if we create space for ourselves and our families to grow. To be fair, I understand that you have to consider your resources. Your family dynamic might be very different from the story I just shared, and I get that. Your kids may not be enthusiastic about online learning. You may find that sixth-grade math is a lot harder than you remember it. Your kids may want to turn off their cameras, and they may feel that they don't want to jump on a video call where they let every kid in the class come into their home. I get that. Because lots of adults feel the same way. Don't you?

Is it really new or revolutionary to say that kids don't want to go to school? Even if school can happen on the couch? It's still school. It's still necessary. And now it's part of the new normal. As I write these words, school districts are trying to decide what the coming year will look like. Schools in Los Angeles County (https://bit.ly/wfh-laschools) are considering a hybrid model, where kids come into the classroom on a reduced schedule during the week. A hybrid school model might mean a full-time work-from-home arrangement – or create some unprecedented childcare concerns during the days when kids are home but parents are not. Debra Duardo, the superintendent for the LA County Office of Education, tells the *Los Angeles Times* that there will be major changes, including kids playing alone, one-way hallways, face coverings, eating lunch at desks, and restrictions on the playground – all of which could be very difficult to enforce in a classroom full of first graders. "Unfortunately, some of the things that children could enjoy in the past, they're not going to be able to do that," Duardo shares. Will these changes translate for other districts nationwide? And how will parents react to the restrictive rules? Will education become another part of working from home? These questions remain a concern for many, with no clear answers in sight.

Keisha Nickolson is a single mom. She's not only the parent of a fifth-grader, she's also a fifth-grade teacher. When she told her daughter, Korinne, that school had been canceled, Korinne just thought that meant another two weeks. "Then I'm going back to see my friends, right?" Korinne asked her mother. It was hard to say what needed to be said: school is done. We're not going back to the building. Keisha tells me that her daughter took a walk in the neighborhood by herself to process that news. She would be heading into sixth grade – a new building – without ever saying goodbye to the old one. There was a lot of letting go, in more ways than one. Because Keisha is a teacher in a district that's different from the one they live in, the two would drive to school together, as they had every day since kindergarten. That tradition – like the end-of-year skating party that Korinne had been looking forward to for the past three years – was history. Graduation? Field Day? Nope. The lockdown from coronavirus canceled all those things. And more.

Although she missed her friends and missed her school, Korinne was able to get online and get her assignments without too much trouble. Meanwhile, Keisha was working harder than ever. A colleague introduced her to the brave new world of Zoom, and she was thrilled to be able to see "her kids" again. But without her

Korinne and Keisha

break room – that place away from students where she could let off steam with her co-workers – she was feeling the pinch of working from home. Texting with colleagues and talking with her principal were huge outlets for her. She also turned to her faith for guidance.

"My superintendent's email signature says, 'Don't focus on what you can't change, focus on what you can,'" Keisha says. "I can't change what got canceled and how I miss my kids in my classroom. What I *can* change is how I respond or react to something. So, either I could meet that change with resistance and say, 'Oh, I don't want to do it!' – just like a kid in my classroom would. Or I could say, 'Okay, what do I know how to do? I know how to teach. I know the content. I know the state's standards. I know the curriculum. I do know that,'" she says, taking a pause. "I had to take what I know and place it into the container of what I don't know, and do the best that I can with that." She's teaching in a way she's never done before, with childcare support of sisters and other family members – plus the firm encouragement of parents who are deeply dedicated to her students' lives.

> "Enjoy the little things, for one day you may look back and realize they were the big things."
> -Robert Brault

> **Vala Afshar** ✓
> @ValaAfshar
>
> The four words you are likely to hear from remarkable leaders:
>
> "How can I help?"

Like most teachers, she keeps a "Smile File": a handy stash of thank-you cards, letters, and mementos that students have given to her over the past several months. She often takes out a hand-written card as a reminder of how she's made a difference – and how she still is. "It's not easy," she says.

Because teaching your own kids isn't easy, even for trained educators, you may want to consider some online resources that can help you with ideas, structure, and options for handling those responsibilities. No matter what your circumstances, or your preferences, consider that working from home, like schooling from home, is a big shift. Some adapt more easily than others.

Maybe you have kids who are younger than the ones in this chapter. Maybe you're a single parent. Maybe you've got triplets. Maybe other parents in your neighborhood would be willing to "combine pods" to help spread out some teaching responsibilities. Homeschool parents have been banding together like this for years.

Don't be afraid to innovate – you don't have to go it alone. Reach out to friends and other parents via text or Zoom – because people in different circumstances are still fighting the same battles. And you can figure this out, just like your kids can. What innovative ideas will work best for you and your family dynamic? Check out the Home + Work section for a summary of high-level ideas for your action plan.

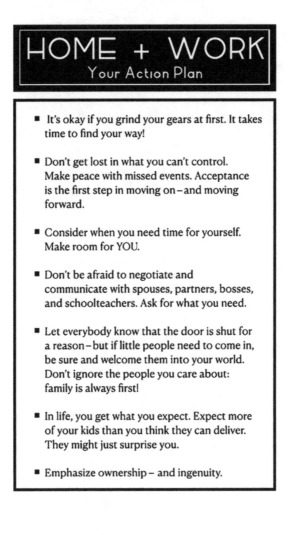

HOME + WORK
Your Action Plan

- It's okay if you grind your gears at first. It takes time to find your way!

- Don't get lost in what you can't control. Make peace with missed events. Acceptance is the first step in moving on – and moving forward.

- Consider when you need time for yourself. Make room for YOU.

- Don't be afraid to negotiate and communicate with spouses, partners, bosses, and schoolteachers. Ask for what you need.

- Let everybody know that the door is shut for a reason – but if little people need to come in, be sure and welcome them into your world. Don't ignore the people you care about: family is always first!

- In life, you get what you expect. Expect more of your kids than you think they can deliver. They might just surprise you.

- Emphasize ownership – and ingenuity.

Redefining Success in the New Normal

H ow do you feel about the phrase "the secrets of success"?

What would happen if success were no longer a secret?

We're all working from home now. Let's get rid of the secrets by busting some of the myths about success. Because success isn't a location. Or something hidden. Especially when it comes to your career. But in order to find what success really means in the new normal, we've got to shatter a few myths.

I asked my friends:

Karen Mangia
@karenmangia

What's the biggest misconception or myth about #success ?

10:27 AM · Nov 14, 2019 · Twitter for iPhone

Here's what they told me:

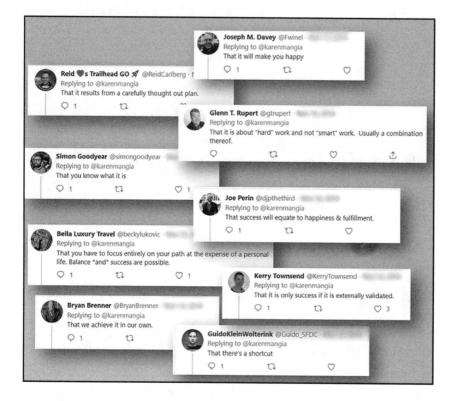

What does success look like in the new normal?

For me, success always looked like something external. Something "out there," reserved for other folks. Maybe it was money, or a job title, or perhaps what looked like the "perfect life" (whatever that is – I'm still not sure). But it was always something just out of reach, and always on a timeline. Or a deadline. Or both.

Managing your calendar makes you efficient. You're able to execute effectively when you manage your time wisely. But what about when the unexpected happens? Your meeting goes long, your boss asks for something unexpected, you find yourself working in your pajamas in the middle of a global pandemic: can you still succeed? Maybe. But the well-thought-out plan is suddenly not so useful anymore. Adaptability is what's needed.

By the way, you know who got all of their New Year's resolutions wrong in 2020?

Everybody.

Setting high goals is part of my DNA; I'll always do it and I'll always try. I hope you aim high, too – because you never know where your goals may lead you.

Sometimes, when I set goals, things go my way. Sometimes they don't. And sometimes – I'm leaning in so that I can whisper this secret to you – I've gotten exactly what I wanted, and it turned out that it didn't feel like success at all. I gained a new hassle instead of a handle on success. Have you been there? Okay. So, let's talk about what success is not:

- Success is not a destination.

- Success is not a location.

- Success is not a number in your bank account. Look again: that number is just a number.

- Success is not your title.

- Success is not an achievement or an award that you receive.

- If other people are telling you what success should be for you, that's not success.

- Success happens one moment at a time.

See, when it comes to success, our timeline is almost always wrong.

We think success is linear, following a pattern, the result of hard work. And success is scheduled to show up on Thursday at 4:00 p.m. Then life happens. Your appointment with success gets moved up, or moved out, or moved onto someone else's calendar.

Here's an example: When I was working on this book, I thought I was losing my mind. I wrote all these chapters, but I didn't feel like the first one was right. The other chapters – even this one – felt right. But not the first one. It was out of sequence! I was stressed. Guess what?

Success doesn't always come in a sequence.

When we let go of our preconceptions about what success looks like, that's when we see it. When success is free to show up in whatever order and at whatever time – even unannounced – that's when it is most welcome.

That's when we go back and rewrite Chapter 1.

Because, when you get right down to it, we don't really know much about success. Because we always think success should have shown up by now.

Have you ever said or heard these phrases before?

- We should be back to work *by now*.
- I should be married *by now*.
- Other people have been promoted to vice president – why hasn't that happened to me *by now*?
- I should be living in Manhattan Beach/driving a fancy car/owning my own business *by now*.

Does any of that sound familiar?

Does any of that sound successful?

No. Not really. Labeling your life with a "by now" tag is a recipe for suffering, not success.

Comments about what should have happened by now shows that we don't know how long it takes to succeed. We don't know when success will arrive – only when we think it *should*.

> "The greatest discovery of all time is that a person can change her future just by changing her attitude."
> -*Oprah Winfrey*

We *should* be able to go back to the way things were. Seniors *should* be allowed to go to the prom. *By now*. What we should be able to do, by now, is a source of either pressure or discouragement. Either option is a choice to make ourselves feel bad, no matter how you slice it. Does it help your performance when you put more pressure on yourself?

How's that pressure and discouragement helping you to succeed? Take two words away from your definition of success and it gets more realistic. More real. More right now.

Subtract "*by now*," and you're on to something.

How many times has success come out of nowhere? You were working hard, over there, and then when success showed up over here ... it was (dare I say it?) effortless. You struggle and strive to make the fabulous dinner party and put in all the work. Then your friends show up, the cake is baked, the wine is poured, and then, you realize something: success is an experience that goes beyond effort.

In a conversation I had with Jeanenne Ray, at Wiley, we were chatting about the manuscript I had just turned in – the manuscript for *Listen Up!*, which will interestingly be published about 60 days after the book you're reading right now. I was explaining my focus on working from home, how I had been blogging on the subject on ZDNet and elsewhere, as part of my efforts to help over 50,000 employees make the transition from offices all around the globe. Jeanenne asked me if I would consider pulling my thoughts together into a book. This book. The one you are reading right now.

The conversation came out of nowhere and led me somewhere: to a place where my ideas and words are literally in your hands (or in your ears, via audio).

Success shows up in a conversation. In a moment. Maybe it comes from hard work; more often it comes beside it or behind it or because of it. But when it shows up, you find yourself saying "why not?" more easily than ever before. That's how this book began. It started with a moment of success – a conversation that created a choice. Then a direction. And ultimately, a creation.

An old friend used to tell me his constant prayer: "May I have what I want and want what I have." Actually, that guy figured out how to answer his own prayer. When he realized success isn't a thing or a timeline, he saw that it's already here.

What would success look like to you, right now? What if there were no timeline attached to success? What would that look like for you? I'm asking if you can define success, on your own terms, in this moment. In this place. Wherever you are right now, can you find success – even in your home office?

> "The only limitation to our realization of tomorrow will be our doubts of today."
> -*Franklin D. Roosevelt*

Here's what success feels like to me: it feels like I'm learning and growing and finding new ways of looking at the same old problems. I may not hit my goal, or meet every step in my plan. Then again, I might crush my calendar and blow my goals out of the water. Who knows? But success, in this moment, feels like the ability to choose. To adapt and to act in accordance with what makes the most sense for me, right now. How about you?

I can't always choose my circumstances, but I can always choose how I respond to them. I can choose to be under pressure and discouraged. Or I can choose to play full out: being fully present and engaged with the relationships that matter, the work that matters, the things that I care about. What would happen if you played the game full out – as best you could – no matter what it was that you were tackling? Or where you were playing the game?

Sometimes I feel a sense of overwhelm: *Oh my god, how am I going to get this done?* Other times, I say, *thank god I can get this done!* My workload might be the same. But the way I go about moving through life is different. The response is what changes. The response is my moment-to-moment success. The response is the mindset that matters.

I've spent a lifetime learning what I'm about to share with you right now. The key to more success is actually less.

Less obligation. Less commitment. Less overreacting. Less pressure. Less discouragement.

When I have less, I get more out of life.

I can hear you saying, "But obligations always exist! Working from home is filled with pressure and deadlines! Circumstances are never exactly as we wish! There's always stuff we have to do!"

I hear you. I know the feeling. And I know something else. There's a mindset that can make a difference.

When we bring less baggage to the game of life – and the game of working from home – we're free to do more with what we've been given. Even if we're being forced into a makeshift home office during the most dangerous pandemic that we've seen in our lifetimes, we can adapt to the unplanned. We can even thrive in it, if we take time to consider what success really looks like. Our circumstances may not be ideal – but we can always choose how to react.

Don't wait on success. Choose it, right now, and you'll find it one moment at a time. Given that there are things that need to be done, is it helping you to put more pressure on yourself and the situation? Given your circumstances, does discouragement help move you forward? No. The mindset of letting go is the mindset of choice – and the first step toward action. What are you waiting for?

Surprisingly, time and time again I hear of people finding joy in working from home. Unexpected productivity. Unplanned success.

> **Vala Afshar** ✔
> @ValaAfshar
>
> "As I look back on my life, I realize that every time I thought I was being rejected from something good, I was actually being re-directed to something better."

And that's amazing to me, because I like to plan everything. In different times, I loved to plan for an elaborate dinner party: planning the menus, planning the guests, planning the invitations – it was both fun and nerve-wracking at the same time, creating this magical and fabulous experience. Plus, my name, Mangia, means "to eat" in Italian. So, the way I was raised, when someone shows up at your house, you're culturally required to feed them. I mean, they could have just come from a buffet lunch. It could be 10 minutes after Thanksgiving dinner. I don't care. All I want to know is, can I get you something to eat?

My boyfriend, Eric, was hanging out and having a social distance visit with one of his fraternity brothers, who's also a friend of mine. We live in a downtown neighborhood where it's easy to walk to several nearby pubs and restaurants. After sampling one of the local spots, these two gents decided to walk back to the house. I found them sitting on the back patio and swapping stories.

I stepped out the back door to say hello. That was when my Italian DNA kicked in. Instantly, I realized I should make a snack. Right? Maybe even a meal. Before you could say, *bongiorno*, I said, "Hey, are you guys hungry?"

Their response sent me inside, into the kitchen. That's when I realized: I have no plan!

I opened the cabinets and the refrigerator. I began with a quick inventory: What have I got to work with? If I roll up this sliced turkey, and stick it on a nice board next to some cheese, it will look like a poor man's charcuterie plate. I found the Cheez-Its® and I grabbed the snack mix we like from Trader Joe's. I poured these things into bowls, stuck spoons in there somewhere, opened a bag of nuts, poured them in a bowl. I took it all outside, along with three forks, three drinks, and three plates: here you go.

Later, after much chewing and conversation, Eric and his friend could only say one thing: the food was *amazing*.

What? I didn't plan on hearing that response.

Now, I'm a trained chef, and a champion of preparation, yet I had used none of my superpowers to create this so-called amazing meal. Were they patronizing me? Trying to butter me up or something? I wanted to argue with both of these guys. But I couldn't. Because they were right.

The amazing meal wasn't about planning or ingredients or presentation or my stellar culinary skills. What made the evening so delicious was the connection we felt around the conversation.

And please don't tell anyone, or ring my doorbell right now, but I had fun pulling together the bits at the last minute.

After it was all said and done, I realized that success was about finding ways to make the most of what you have. The connection was what mattered; the food was secondary. By contrast, I have spent days and weeks on end planning elaborate dinners that are delicious and fabulous but get this: I don't enjoy them as much as that simple snackfest I made in a moment in my backyard.

Success showed up when I just walked up to the cabinets and said, "Hello!" Then I said, whatever, boom, here's a spoon, take it outside. In that instant, my choice freed up all my energy to just hang out and spend it having a conversation. The absence of planning meant the presence of connection. Less planning actually meant a lot more. Especially when I trusted myself and just started reaching into my cabinets.

A makeshift meal is a lot like working from home. We use what we have. We innovate and reach out for new ideas. Then, somehow, success shows up – but only when we see it one moment at a time: inside a conversation, in a child's eyes, or a partner's touch. Even inside a box of Cheez-Its. Don't believe me? Put down your calendar and look again.

Too much time spent orchestrating and planning and trying to force the plan robs you of your energy – energy that can be spent enjoying the moment. *Success happens one moment at a time.* Turn off the timetable and you're instantly more successful. Hopefully you've realized that *by now*? :-)

They say that home is where the heart is – now it's also where you work. And where you will succeed.

Choosing how I respond to circumstances – even if those circumstances aren't exactly what I might want – is really what success looks like. Even if I have to work from home and wear a mask and wait to go into the grocery store. Even if the kids want to come in during a video call and the dog just barfed on the carpet and my boss has an unplanned emergency for me. I can still choose how I respond to those situations. I can still choose success.

As near as I can tell, success is about freedom. Freedom from what others say success really is. Freedom – and permission – to say "no" to the things that don't serve you. Freedom from the timelines and obligations that others give us. Or, if you're like me, the obligations we put on ourselves.

When I worked in sales, I was working a bazillion hours per week. Eventually my hard work paid off: I sold the largest, multimillion-dollar sale that our branch had ever made. Taking a customer from spending nothing to becoming the largest deal for any rep in my entire region made me a local hero. My manager congratulated me publicly. Then he told me a secret privately. A secret I will never forget.

Dave, my manager, asked me to step into his office. "Here's what's amazing about you," he began. "I know if I ask you to do something – anything – you will push that 500-pound rock up the mountain. It will absolutely get there – I have no question about that." He shut the door to his office and turned back to face me. "The part that you're not getting is that you're killing yourself moving that boulder. Smart managers know how to break that 500-pound rock into smaller pieces. Then they have other people join them on the journey up the mountain." He was sitting at his desk now.

"Success isn't about repetitively demonstrating that you can push harder, so that you can shove heavier rocks up higher hills. Success is demonstrating that you can get other people to join you in your charge. Otherwise, you're going to wear yourself out." I remember him twisting a black and silver pen between his fingers, before he looked up at me. "What if you could do that?" he asked, referring to the ability to break things down into simpler smaller parts and get others to help shoulder the load. "What if you could have been working *two* of the hugest deals we've ever seen, instead of just one?"

Success is best when you spread it around. Success is meant to be shared.

Instead of getting lost in what should have happened by now, drop the timeline and start figuring out how to get others involved in your goals and dreams. You may not know how long it takes to succeed, but you do know this: success is closer when you get others to share in the possibilities.

Just because you're not in the office doesn't mean you can't create connection and engagement. Here are three quick work-from-home tips to help you to access success from anywhere.

1. **Delegate:** In the office, it was often wise or politically smart to hang on to work. That way, you could pass it along to your boss or your leadership team and obtain praise and recognition for what you brought to them. Now, the office dynamic has changed. Collaboration is the new political capital. Sharing and distribution is the centerpiece of the high-performance mindset. Break up that boulder into smaller pieces and get others to help you reach the top of the mountain. Provide opportunities around your initiatives that make sense for the people you need – so that your supporters see their success in your vision. There's never been a greater need for connection, inclusion, and teamwork. What can you do, right now, to delegate, distribute, and engage your team? Don't just hang on to your boulder and try to move it all by yourself!

2. **Communicate:** Have you got the coverage you need, so that you can concentrate on what matters most? Be clear about what that looks like: if you need extra time for child-care stuff, share that request with your boss. Let your partner and your kids know what your schedule looks like and see what they can do to help you in your new normal. But don't forget to communicate how you can help others: What coverage can you provide to your boss, your teammates, your significant other? Communication is a two-way street! And when your kids bust into the office, communicate that you care by letting them into your world. Don't try to push them away, like some of the memes we've seen. Family matters, so bring them into your world. Why not? Besides, any kid is going to get completely bored by a work conference call after two minutes. But they are there because they need you. They need you to help them find their success! What can

you share with your boss, your team, and your family that can help you to get what you need? And if you're not clear on exactly what that is, remember: listening is an important part of communication!

3. **Innovate:** Trying to shoehorn the old ways into the new normal is a fool's errand. The world has changed; have you? What are you doing to take a fresh look at the way business gets done? How are you establishing regular channels of two-way communication, so that you (and your team and your company) can better adapt to what's needed, now?

The future belongs to the people and the companies that are able to pivot, reimagine, and move forward. The mindset of success starts with acceptance: accepting where we are, today. Taking that first step forward, in the spirit of greater communication, delegation, and innovation, points toward better days ahead. In the next chapter, I'll share some surprising stories of innovative companies (and individuals) who have found new ways to reinvent.

Accessing Innovation

Where does innovation come from?

When we default to what we already know, instead of being inspired to discover what's possible, innovation ceases to exist. For entrepreneurs, innovation is the key to survival. After all, the most dangerous seven words in business are "that's the way we've always done things." With the arrival of the global pandemic, the new normal opens the door for innovation and reinvention.

Certain business sectors have been hit hard in the new normal: air travel, car rental, retail shops, and more. One market that has been almost entirely wiped off the planet is live events. Conferences are big business: Allied Research (https://bit.ly /wfh-alliedresearch) says that the live event industry was valued at $1.1 billion in 2018, with projections to grow to $2.3 billion by 2026. (I'm guessing those projections have since received a revision. What's your bet?) In the past, according to Convene (https://bit.ly/wfh-convene), there were 1.9 million meetings annually (more than 5,200 every single day). Those 1.9 million meetings resulted in some big spending. If you add up planning, production, travel, and other direct expenditures, meetings and events account for $325 billion of direct spending (https://bit.ly /wfh-meetingbiz) in the United States. What are event companies going to do to take their business virtual? Can you really have an effective conference in the cloud? And a more important question: How do you define a "virtual event experience"?

Answering that question points us toward another shift. Innovation isn't just a concept in the new normal: it's a requirement.

That's according to Bari Baumgardner, the founder of SAGE Event Management – a live events company she founded in 2004 in North Carolina. (SAGE stands for "Strategic Advice for Growing Events.") When the world went virtual, SAGE (https://poweredbysage.com/) had to adapt in order to survive. The business was based on people connecting in person, traveling (often via airplane) to a destination event. Bari had to answer a question that every company was asking: Is there a way to replicate the event experience online? Because, in a virtual economy, experience is the new currency.

Together with her husband and business partner, Blue Melnick, Bari pivoted to virtual events. She wasn't sure if the audience would go online with her.

The team had two weeks to pivot their first in-person event to a virtual event experience. The pitch was simple. "Let's experiment together," they told their clients. And it worked.

One of the first to agree was a trade association. Their event was scheduled over a three-day weekend. This group of CEOs had met annually for over 25 years, so recreating that three-day experience was going to be a challenge. "We decided what the attendees really needed was a break at the end of the day. We scheduled a cocktail conversation every other week for 10 weeks," Bari says. The innovation transformed the event, shifted the timeline, and provided the virtual experience that had been missing in the past. The reviews were outstanding, and Bari reports that the execs have never been happier.

SAGE also caters to information marketing events, in addition to corporate work, serving an elite group of keynote speakers, authors, and knowledge brokers: "It's a niche area where influencers can create a purpose-driven event," she explains. And a purpose-driven payday. Purpose-driven events are aspirational gatherings where attendees are exposed to some version of their higher selves – through skills training, personal development, or some form of business development guidance. People buy tickets to these events and are typically presented with an opportunity to receive extended support to help them achieve their goals, via a high-ticket offer from the company or entrepreneur. These offers can range from the low four figures up to $15,000 - or more.

For certain entrepreneurs and organizations, these multiday events can bring in six, seven, or even eight figures. How do you capture that kind of business if you can't be in the same room with your clients and prospects?

"On average, we're seeing three to four times the number of attendees at virtual events," Bari explains, citing the ease of access and the appeal of being able to join from your home office, no travel required. She had an event scheduled in Indianapolis that would have brought 300 people to the city. The online event served four times more attendees and grossed 20% more than the year before. "But here's the thing: *the net was so much higher*," Bari explains, citing the reduced costs and overhead. An event in Orlando had brought in 1,000 people and $2.5 million last year, pre-COVID. When they shifted it to an online format, attendance tripled and so did gross revenues. How is that even possible?

"The biggest mistake that people make is treating a virtual event like a webinar," Bari says from inside her studio facility. Indeed, when you say "virtual event," people think livestream, webinar, or teleseminar – don't you?

But referencing what you think something is won't help you to reimagine it.

Innovation doesn't come from what you already know. Bari, Blue, and the team tapped into these five words to begin their exploration: "What else could this be?"

Their first thought was to find a powerful new online platform. There are many choices out there: Bizzabo, Socio, On24, Glisser, Eventtia, Sococo, Whova, Boomset, Brella, Pathable, vFairs, Virbela . . . but all of them have a bit of a learning curve, as you enter their various virtual worlds. Simplicity was the goal. They wanted as little learning as possible, in order to drive participation and engagement. So, her choice? Zoom.

Using the familiar Zoom format, SAGE has changed the way that people show up, stay engaged, and get motivated using their online setup. To be fair, they've got an elaborate studio, switching equipment, and multiple cameras – but the studio they built goes beyond gadgets. Turns out you don't have to have a super-expensive studio in order to create real value in an online event. There's no price tag on innovation. In fact, how much you choose to spend can also be part of your reinvention.

Here are the four components of getting people to show up – and stick around – for a virtual event experience:

1. **No Recordings:** "We looked at what people allow in 'virtual world' that they do not allow in an in-person world," Bari explains, tapping into her 25-year experience in the live events industry. "If you come to an in-person event, and you miss a session because you step out to take a call or you show up late, you don't get access to that session." There's no recording – you have to be present to access the information. How can you do that in a virtual event? "We made the decision that there would not be replays because we want to distinguish this event from a webinar or a telesummit where it's easy to get access to a replay or the recordings," she shares. Step out and you're going to miss out, it's that simple. "That's what we wanted to duplicate for our live events so

that we could get people to understand that if they wanted to take advantage of that content, connection, and community, they had to be in the virtual room where it happens in order to gain access." The result? The policy drove unprecedented show-up rates and participation. Clients market the event to let people know that there are no recordings.

2. **The Swag Box:** When's the last time you were getting ready for an online event and the FedEx guy showed up at your door with a box of presents and branded gifts to help you prepare for what's ahead? Bari says with a hint of disappointment in her voice, "You don't get gifts with a telesummit or teleseminar or webinar." But with SAGE, she says with a smile, the Swag Box is a special delivery designed to drive engagement, branding, and participation. Bari asks, "What's the absolute best email reminder you could get to show up for a virtual event?" Answer: NOT an email. There are too many emails these days. And when you get a box of gifts there's an element of both intrigue and reciprocity. A physical gift welcomes you to the virtual world. People feel like if they've already received gifts, they'd better show up. And they're curious about the content – because if this box is what happens before the event starts . . . Well, who knows what it's going to be like *during* the event? So, what's in the box? A journal is a great gift, for example. Branded mugs, water bottles, T-shirts, hats, and so on. What are things that you use every day that you think the audience would love, too? What are things/tools that will help your audience to be able to do the work that you need them to do? Put that in the box! Looking for ideas? Just do a Google search for "branded product" or "branded material." Also: get one great thing instead of 10 not-so-great things, Bari says. "Make it intentional. It says a lot about your brand and the experience they're going to have with you."

3. **In-Person Check-In:** When you sign up for a virtual event produced by SAGE, the process is a little different. The Zoom invitation you receive is for an online tech check-in, not the meeting itself. "Every live event has in-person registration. Because you wouldn't let someone into your ballroom without having a badge on. Why would you let them into your virtual event without having done the same thing?" Bari asks. For a 3,000-person event, invites were sent out, segmented by time frame, for the registration process. Two days before the event, Bari had the team sitting in various Zoom rooms to get everyone checked in. The team had a crystal-clear agenda for the check-ins. Because when the virtual event starts, they want to start strong. Have you been on a call where you spend the first 30 minutes doing technology checks? You know the drill: "No, Taylor, I can't see you. Sorry, Karen – how do I unmute myself? Oops, that was the dog!" Ugh. Nobody wants that. Bari explains the Zoom room registration like this: "All attendees had to actually say hello (on camera and on mic) to a member of our staff. We walked them through a series of questions and instructions. 'Can you raise your hand? Can you mute yourself?'" The first contact married tech and touch, just to reconfirm that attendees will be using the camera, raising hands, using the chat window . . . that sort of thing. What happens when a virtual conference starts off with connection, even before it begins? Bari reveals their intentions. "In the Zoom room registrations, if more than one person showed up at a time, our team was instructed to introduce attendees to one another. So right away, we're starting to get people connected, plus doing the tech check together." The real impact here? The company was able to set expectations, up front. They were

able to tell people how they needed them to show up for the event. Participants met other attendees before the event began – just like you might at a conference registration desk. Because of that connection, there was anticipation and excitement – a sense of caring and camaraderie – like a live event. When the virtual event began, a host (emcee) took the virtual stage and there was a sort of "door opening" ceremony. Nearly 80% of attendees were already there, in the virtual room, with cameras on and microphones muted, about 30 minutes prior to the event start! End result? About 70–80% of all check-ins stayed for the entire three days – a participation stat that's unheard of in live events! (For more on how SAGE is transforming this industry, check out this YouTube video featuring Bari and her husband, Blue Melnick: https://bit.ly/wfh-sage).

4. **Fun-ification:** Bari explains fun-ification as a combination of gamification and fun, encouraging interaction wherever possible. "Fun-ification is rewarding people for taking actions that you want them to take." For example: showing up, sharing a post, clicking on a sponsor area, or interacting with vendors can get you points, or praise, or both. Bari's team created a point system and a leaderboard to track things, so people could see how they were progressing in real time. However, you don't have to go to all that trouble, she says. You could simply set up a Facebook group at no cost and, during or after a session, encourage people to post their biggest "Aha!" moment from the conference. And when you see them posting, reward them for it – with a shout-out from the presenter, or additional swag, or both. Create excitement around the behavior. "We didn't tell people we were giving them points just for checking in. But attendees would post in the Facebook group, "oh wow

guys you get points for check-in" and it built up organic encouragement. The Facebook posts were plentiful: "You have to check in, and check it out!" At the end of the conference, having some really great prizes for those at the top of the leaderboard encouraged participation and kept people sticking around to the end. "You want to reward the folks that have stuck with you and played full-out," Bari says, with a quick smile. Because, let's face it: virtual events *are* live events. They're just delivered differently.

You don't have to be handling 3,000 check-ins and multimillion-dollar revenues in order to have a powerful virtual event. But you do have to access innovation. Smart companies will hire a professional emcee – someone who knows the ins and outs of the virtual platform. I'm not saying that your comptroller can't handle the microphone. I'm just suggesting there's a better way. Being deliberate about your delivery is more important than ever, in a work-from-home world.

Delivery has been the key to success for Joseph Davey. He's a former restaurateur turned entrepreneur – and the first registered sommelier in the State of Indiana. He's the General Manager at Vine and Table, a high-end establishment that he says is more than just a wine shop.

"I don't think of my customers as customers. I think of them as guests," Joseph says. So how could he serve his guests when a vital part of his business was sidelined during the quarantine? I'm talking about the gold standard in his industry: the ever-present wine tasting.

Instead of inviting guests to the store for a physical wine tasting experience, he flipped his business model. His wine tastings now offer guests the opportunity to prebuy the wine or to taste along with wines they've already purchased. Then, Joseph hosts an online event with the winemaker on Zoom. He handles bourbon and whisky tastings the same way. Seems like a smart play, in terms of cash flow: you get your money up front. But what if folks don't like the wine?

"It's not really a cash flow play. We're owned by one of the largest liquor distribution companies in Indiana," he says, referring to Big Red Liquors. The company operates about 60 stores across the state from their headquarters in Indianapolis. "So it's not really about getting money up front. It's about service," Joseph shares, explaining why he was one of the first in the city to do virtual tastings.

Past Relationships, Present Value

If you don't like what you've got, he takes the wine back. Same for spirits. He notes what he learns about guests and their preferences, and sends them something they will enjoy more. "I'm pretty good at finding out exactly what fits for someone's tastes," he says, with a nod of his head and a recommendation that I try a particular Riesling that he thinks I will enjoy.

He's turned his attention to social media as well, creating a video series called "How to Cocktail." He invites local restaurant owners onto the program and films them making their most famous cocktails – the ones that the restaurant is offering for carry-out. He builds his own brand when the content is shared by the restaurant, creating goodwill for Vine and Table. Meanwhile, he's driving sales for the featured liquors with a DIY message that doesn't take away from the restaurants. It's a win-win for everyone involved.

His mission statement is bringing a fine-dining level of hospitality and service to specialty retail. Joseph says that statement informs every aspect of his business. So, when he had to figure out how to do curbside orders, he ran the idea through the filter of his mission statement. "We do curbside at the highest level of service possible," he says without hesitation. Pickups are scheduled online, but if you pull up into the parking lot and call the store, someone will take your call – and they will make your order a priority. Because that's service at the highest level possible.

Circumstances have changed in the work-from-home world. But good service is still good service. People crave bespoke and tailored experiences, whether in virtual meetings or virtual wine tastings. The new normal must be redesigned and reimagined around the needs that we all have. Because those needs haven't gone away, and they never will. However, the way we deliver and connect and serve has changed.

According to a 2018 survey from PWC (https://bit.ly /wfh-pwcsurvey), nearly 80% of CEOs struggle to find these two skills: creativity and innovation. Those were the two most-desired capabilities in the survey. Today, consistent performance means consistently embracing variables. And 100% of organizations need to be more creative and more innovative than ever before.

What's your roadmap to innovation? See the following image for some ideas you can use, today, to help find creative solutions in the new normal.

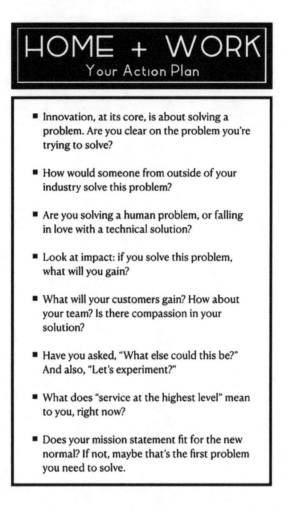

HOME + WORK
Your Action Plan

- Innovation, at its core, is about solving a problem. Are you clear on the problem you're trying to solve?

- How would someone from outside of your industry solve this problem?

- Are you solving a human problem, or falling in love with a technical solution?

- Look at impact: if you solve this problem, what will you gain?

- What will your customers gain? How about your team? Is there compassion in your solution?

- Have you asked, "What else could this be?" And also, "Let's experiment?"

- What does "service at the highest level" mean to you, right now?

- Does your mission statement fit for the new normal? If not, maybe that's the first problem you need to solve.

Creating the High-Performance Remote Work Culture

Twitter made global headlines when CEO Jack Dorsey announced that all employees could work from home, forever (https://bit.ly/wfh-twitterannouncement). On a Friday afternoon, just prior to the announcement, James Loduca was brought in to develop a playbook that would be used globally for the company's 5,300 employees. The announcement that working from home would be permanent, if employees wanted it, was made on the following Monday. Loduca is the Director of Global Inclusion and Diversity at Twitter; I caught up with him via video call in his San Francisco home office.

Loduca, in a black T-shirt that matches the color of his glasses, is petting a penguin. Actually, several penguins, on the gray onesie his 10-week-old son is wearing. Baby Gus (and his adorable onesie) are being held and bounced as Loduca explains Twitter's transition to a work-from-home culture.

"We're really fortunate in that Twitter decided long ago that the future of work was distributed. Our mission is to enable anyone, anywhere, to work for Twitter, which is really at its core about decentralization, diversity, and inclusion. The study of Tweeps' needs for working from home," he says, referencing the company's name for its employees, "had been completed before the pandemic. So it wasn't like we were starting from scratch."

James kick-started the company's new initiative with some deep listening to employees.

When you want to work out what a work-from-home culture looks like, you've got to have a variety of people at the table for that discussion. He says you've got to uncover how a diverse and dispersed workforce is affected by this new normal – because one size does not fit all. "We knew immediately, for example, if you were a primary caregiver [for a child] during the pandemic, and we were transitioning you to shelter in place, you were going to need help. We made productivity allowances and expanded our child-care allowance. Then, the schools closed. So, our plans to help with child care weren't a fit anymore." The company isn't afraid to launch new programs – and quickly let them go, if they don't create results. "We did a listening session. We heard a need for greater flexibility."

James shares how the company responded in the early days of the lockdown. "We acknowledged up front that a global pandemic is going to impact productivity. So we immediately paused all performance ratings. Instead, we shipped tools to managers to allow them to do more meaningful check-ins, focusing on the mental and physical health of our Tweeps first, and put productivity second." The company leaned in on trust: "Trust people to design their lifestyles," James says, articulating the cure for micromanagement. "Work from anywhere is a tool to deepen, not reduce, trust across teams."

CEO Jack Dorsey and his direct reports model the kind of leadership they'd like to see throughout the organization. James says, "Be intentional about not taking every meeting on camera. Take that call while you're walking around your block. Get some fresh air, get away from your screen, give your eyes a rest.

Give your mind a slight mental reboot," he says. "These micro adjustments can have macro impact on how you feel by the end of the day."

> **Vala Afshar** ✔
> @ValaAfshar
>
> You are not a team because you work together. You are a team because you trust, respect, and care for each other.

The company sets all meetings to start at either five minutes past the hour or 35. Those extra five minutes are designed to give employees time to use the bathroom or make some tea or do whatever is needed. "You'd be surprised what a difference five minutes makes," James says, emphasizing that work-from-home is a sustainable initiative, not a fleeting trend. They've introduced a new standard, a variation on their cultural mantra of "Love Where You Work." The new slogan? Love Where You Work (from Home), which is all about how you cope with the new normal. "We're introducing breakout groups where folks come together and share how things are going – what's working and what's not." By facilitating greater collaboration, even in an informal way, the company is fostering greater productivity, understanding, and engagement.

The thing that companies and employees have to watch out for is the "just one more" syndrome. "The temptation to pour that extra glass of wine and stream that extra show is very real," James confesses. "Now I'm very intentional, so that I'm able to get up before the kids wake up and get my day started with a little 'me' time." Whether it's just one more task, one more email, one more meeting, or one more episode on Netflix, the "just one more" syndrome is just not sustainable.

The hardest part of creating a work-from-home culture might just be understanding the people who are really making it happen. It may seem like senior leadership is where change happens, and strategically that's true. A big-picture focus and top-down modeling for the organization is important. But ultimately, C-suite execs are isolated from most of the day-to-day challenges of working from home. And individual contributors – those working with customers and engaging on the front lines – are still in clearly defined roles during the new normal. In fact, for many individual contributors, what they're doing may not have dramatically changed. The location has shifted but the nature of the work, for the most part, has not.

The real crux of the work-from-home culture falls on the shoulders of those who are caught in the middle – those who are asked to monitor and supervise a workforce that they can't see, while managing up to a leadership team who might not really understand. Do you know what I'm talking about?

I'll never forget the time I received my first offer to manage a team. I was thrilled by the career opportunity. I had been successful as a salesperson. And I was just certain that because I was a successful salesperson, I would also be a successful sales manager.

What I discovered when I got into my new job was an unexpected pressure. The requests came from every direction. I mean, the people above me were constantly pinging me to find out what we were going to sell next. And when we were going to sell it and could we close more? At the same time, my team was needing help with escalations, special pricing, and closing opportunities. The environment became more and more complex, and the skills for sales success were not the same ones I needed to survive the "mid-level mashup" of my new world.

Here's another realization: I discovered that everybody else thought that I was basically doing nothing. How many times have you sat and looked at that manager – the one right above you – and thought, "Ah, I could do their job"? What I learned about being a middle manager is that I never worked harder in my life to have other people think I was doing nothing. Can you relate?

Want to create an authentic work-from-home culture inside of your company? Having a vision is important. Boots on the ground are important. But the most critical role in sustaining a work-from-home company comes from the center. Not the top. Or the bottom. The center is what matters for the future of work.

Middle managers are the first line of defense to keep a pulse on how employees are really doing, how they're feeling, how they're adapting, what they're being able to successfully accomplish. The center is where your organization needs to focus, if you want to develop a sustainable culture of engagement, high performance, and trust.

Creating a groundswell of feedback is crucial – that's the deep listening that James Loduca delivered at Twitter. That listening begins inside the ranks of middle management. Because your managers aren't sitting there doing nothing. Actually, they're doing everything.

Laurel Farrer is the President of the Work From Home Association, and the CEO of Distribute Consulting, one of the top firms for work-from-home initiatives. Her company provides a variety of resources on change management and communication – part of a three-legged stool that successful companies use to build successful remote workforce initiatives. "Culture, communications, and trust," she says, are the foundation of a distributed culture that works. And figuring out that combination can impact everything from socioeconomics to diversity to climate issues. Laurel shares that 14 of the 17 United Nations' Sustainable Development Goals can be solved by remote work. But finding the path to those benefits starts in the middle. "Allowing people to change their workplace is totally different from enabling a virtual-friendly organization. That's dependent on infrastructure and operational change," she says.

"Overcommunication is just communication, when people are working from home. The irony is that, in an office environment, we're subconsciously taught to just sit down and shut up and get to work. We stay relevant through nonverbal communication. Now, all of a sudden, our communication needs become very different," Laurel shares. We can't show our work in quite the same way in a remote environment. "Our communication needs have changed: we need to become more articulate in both verbal and written communication." And, I might add, we all need to speak a language called Zoom.

The key for middle manager success is understanding the role that culture plays in a distributed organization. "Culture is not perks," Laurel shares. "It's not a process. It's not proximity. Culture is *personality*. People are able to connect with that corporate personality just as we click with individual personalities. And," she adds, "you don't have to be in the same room with somebody in order to connect with them."

Most companies don't know what a connected culture looks like. As a result, some middle managers are scrambling to find their way. Trust is the first thing that gets dismissed.

Consider this recent quote from *Forbes* (https://bit.ly/wfh -laurelfarrer), where Laurel is a regular contributor:

> *Imagine sending this email to your work-from-home workforce: "We are watching you. We are capturing your keystrokes. We are logging the websites you visit. So get to work – or face the consequences."*

That's a version of an actual email that Axos Financial sent to its remote workers, as reported by the *LA Times*. Many tools are powering the work-from-home revolution, including the surveillance software that's flying off the shelves. Monitoring solutions like InterGuard, Time Doctor, Teramind, ActivTrak, and Hubstaff are thriving in a what-are-you-up-to world. "For some organizations," Laurel says, elaborating on a climate of mistrust, "the current reporting method is that remote workers are required to call their supervisor at the top of every hour and report on what they've done in the past 60 minutes." While it's true that's what gets measured gets done, going keystroke by website by minute isn't always the best way to drive results. Or the most efficient.

So how do middle managers learn to measure, and trust, in a work-from-home world? Has your company had that conversation?

- Are your employees and managers encouraged to work autonomously?
- Does your organization have reporting processes and tools in place to monitor (but not necessarily spy on) your workers?
- What's your cultural context for listening and engaging teams in a distributed environment?

"You need to know what your employees' output is," Laurel says, flatly. "That's not going to change." But how you empower that output is the key to your entire organization's success.

Tuning in to middle management is vital for senior leaders who are in the position of setting strategy, allocating funding, and alleviating challenges. Want more from your individual contributors? Empower your mid-level managers. The ripple effect will translate, helping everyone to perform at their best and deliver the results that the business needs.

So, how do you do that?

First, for middle managers to be successful, they have to own that process. Managers must commit to innovation in order to develop themselves. Managers need to lean in on their careers and reflect on what they need in order to be successful. While strategic guidance, training, and investment can help, managers must invest in themselves. Because when that senior executive asks for management input, managers need to be able to clearly articulate the kind of training and support that will enable success.

I'm talking about innovative training programs: programs designed to help people remotely manage both up and down, programs built around effective video communications, programs assembled around mindfulness and well-being during this global pandemic. How else can managers battle their own burnout and recognize the signs for members of their teams?

A leader is one who knows the way, goes the way, and shows the way, as John Maxwell famously said. Leadership training is the key:

- Training on communication skills.
- Training on how to conduct meetings in the new normal.
- Training on every concept expressed in this book and a forum for greater discussion.
- Looking for ideas? There are lots of training resources on virtuallyperfekt.com and you can find out about Laurel's consulting services at http://distributeconsulting.com.

So often, the middle is overlooked when it comes to training. I'm not talking about quantity – I'm talking about quality. A new quality of management training is what's required, especially when you consider that programs from six months ago aren't relevant anymore! If your company isn't deliberate about success, how are your middle managers going to succeed? When a team becomes distributed – for perhaps the first time in your company's history – a shift is required: a new investment in reskilling and retooling, so that success radiates from the middle.

> **Vala Afshar** ✔
> @ValaAfshar
>
> The bosses we remember:
>
> 1 provided us safe space to grow
> 2 opened career doors
> 3 protected us during uncertainty
> 4 recognized and rewarded us
> 5 developed us as leaders
> 6 inspired us to stretch higher
> 7 led by example
> 8 told us our work mattered
> 9 forgave us when we made mistakes

Smart companies right now are offering training plus opportunities for their mid-level managers to meet together and share what's working and what's not. How are you equipping and empowering your managers to make the shift? If you want to know where to start your training, try asking yourself (and your managers) this question: How do you know that your employees are actually working?

Want some other mission-critical questions? Here goes:

- How do you put outcome-based programs in place?
- What are the micro-management strategies that have cropped up, like weeds in a garden, and need to be pulled?
- How do managers communicate differently in a distributed and a remote environment?
- How do middle managers communicate up the chain when there's either a win or a challenge? After all, no one is walking into the CEO's office when she's at home (like the rest of us).
- How does the leadership team allow for accessibility, while at the same time encouraging crosstalk among the management team?
- What happens to corrective conversations, or performance evaluations, or additional instruction for your team, when a manager can't physically meet with his or her people?
- Are your employees clear on what they can do to communicate greater needs or additional flexibility? What does that process look like in your organization, and how are you equipping managers to say yes to requests (and build loyalty in the process)?

Don't let managers get pinched in the new normal: the work-from-home culture rests on their shoulders, more so than ever before.

- Communication is currency.
- Collaboration is crucial.
- Selfishness around information is sabotage.

Finally, time management has never been more important. Rituals, routines, and boundaries need to be put into a deliberate context, to allow managers to avoid the "just one more" syndrome. I'm talking about efficiency, of course, but I'm also talking about burnout. Because managers can burn the candle on both ends better than anybody. When you're a manager caring for your team, caring for your leadership, caring for your family, I wonder: Who's taking time to care about you? Typically, it's not your calendar. Unless you understand how to manage your time more effectively, burnout is going to creep into your world.

Laurel explains that any change initiative, whether it's changing your coffee vendor or your company culture, comes with a honeymoon period. At first, people say "wow" to working from home. The benefits are many. "But what's happened is that we have been thrown into such an extreme change, so quickly, and extreme change can trigger extreme reactions," she says. A quick glance at the news immediately confirms her findings. "There are changes happening in society that the infrastructure of the country hasn't even caught up with," she explains. "There's no precedent for how the company reacted during the last global pandemic. And people are still discovering the balancing act of managing their children's education and a full-time job and all of the other obligations of life." The wow is wearing off, as the honeymoon turns into the daily operations of the business. Bottom line, critical-thinking skills are what's needed, if companies are going to move to a lasting model. What does sustainability and a long-term work-from-home plan look like – for your company, your team, your culture?

As I've shared in ZDNet, success starts with your story. Considering how self-management and communication will play out on an individual level is the first step in enabling your managers to act on that vision. And every employee needs to participate in crafting that story, both individually and collectively.

> **Vala Afshar** ✔
> @ValaAfshar
>
> No matter how educated, talented, or rich you are, how you treat people ultimately tells all.

Meanwhile, in the midst of all this juggling, there's an even bigger challenge for career-conscious middle managers. In the new normal, the measures of success become murky.

- Are managers measured by those employee pulse survey results from the team?
- Are managers measured by how well the team is actually performing against expectations?
- Are managers measured on the perception of senior leaders?
- Serving multiple masters means that your calendar can get very full: multiple meetings, multiple responsibilities, murky instructions. What's really most important for your organization? And, for managers: Have you built your calendar to support those goals?

As I've said so many times, if everything is important then nothing is. The effective work-from-home culture needs crystal-clear expectations about the outcomes middle managers are supposed to deliver. I believe that managers need a way to connect with their peers and to share ideas about how to stay engaged with their teams and how to affect perception.

And lastly, senior leaders need to focus most on middle managers, if your company cares about burnout. If people on your team are grinding their gears and feeling the frustration, those feelings will be most acute among mid-level managers.

I know from my own experience: it's incredibly easy to feel like you are invisible in the middle. Add the isolation that often comes from remote work, and the potential for burnout is high – that's why there's so much churn in the middle. Many managers move out of the role to escape the added pressure.

Management methodology and mindsets must be updated. Instead of overcompensating and overcontrolling, managers need to be encouraged to see things in a new way. Starting with themselves.

If managers are working hard and perhaps even delivering phenomenal results, how does your company recognize their efforts? Look, don't get me wrong. I realize that everyone's working hard. Statistically speaking, remote workers put in two to four hours (https://bit.ly/wfh-extrahours) more per day than they did in the office. But when managers aren't just working hard, they're working smart, that's an aspect of your culture that needs to be recognized. Shared. Duplicated.

Ask yourself: Are new results being seen, recognized, and rewarded? If so, how? More importantly: Are your management challenges being addressed effectively?

Here are two Home + Work charts, one for managers and the other for corporate leaders that support them. What are you going to do, today, to battle burnout and include the critical members of your team in creating a work-from-home culture?

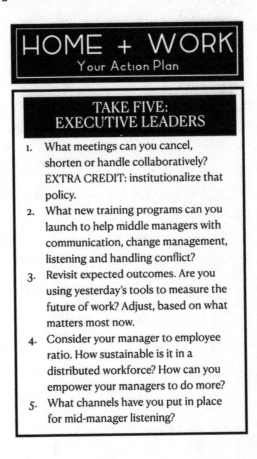

HOME + WORK
Your Action Plan

TAKE FIVE: EXECUTIVE LEADERS

1. What meetings can you cancel, shorten or handle collaboratively? EXTRA CREDIT: institutionalize that policy.

2. What new training programs can you launch to help middle managers with communication, change management, listening and handling conflict?

3. Revisit expected outcomes. Are you using yesterday's tools to measure the future of work? Adjust, based on what matters most now.

4. Consider your manager to employee ratio. How sustainable is it in a distributed workforce? How can you empower your managers to do more?

5. What channels have you put in place for mid-manager listening?

TAKE FIVE: MANAGERS/DIRECTORS

1. What's the biggest challenge you're trying to solve right now? Ask for what you need and say why you need it.

2. How can you engage your employees in solving the challenges the team faces?

3. Try the buddy system. Who's your peer partner? Who's there to listen to you?

4. Get a mentor or coach. Do you have a formal program in place?

5. Ask every team member, in a one-on-one meeting, "What could we do, together, to make this easier for you?" It's not a session for granting wishes - it's an opportunity for listening and gaining agreement around what needs to be done.

10

Career Guidance and Job Search Strategies

As I write these words, 62% of the US workforce is working remotely – 80% of these folks started doing so since the onset of the COVID-19 pandemic, according to a Salesforce survey (https://bit.ly/wfh-salesforceresearch1). Nearly 70% of US workers are interested in working remotely for the long term. In many industries, career change is the focus for about half of the population. From 47% of workers in manufacturing to 52% in hard-hit sectors like transportation and hospitality, finding a new job is top of mind for many.

As I write these words, the unemployment rate continues in the double digits, and leading authorities state that the recent jobless rate of 14% is actually understated (https://bit.ly/wfh -understated). Indeed, *Forbes* senior contributor Chuck Jones says that the actual numbers are meeting or exceeding what was seen during the Great Depression (https://bit.ly/31id7Ef). Even the folks who are employed are still on shaky ground: 57% of millennials are concerned about losing their current positions.

As I write these words, it appears that industries like travel, tourism, and the restaurant industry may never be the same. That prediction goes for many other market segments as well. While the majority of the US workforce (53%) believe they could easily find a new position in their current role or industry, now is a difficult time to try those odds.

However, and this is a big "however," there are opportunities in every economy. Now may be the time when, out of necessity or desire, you wish to move into another position. What does that shift look like, when you're working from home and changing your work?

In an increasingly tight job market, connection is king. And referral is the currency of choice.

> **Vala Afshar** ✔
> @ValaAfshar
>
> You will not remember how much money you made throughout your career.
>
> However, you will remember every single person that graciously opened a career door for you.
>
> Opening doors for others is important and meaningful work. Be a door opener. Be remembered.

If you're trying to find your next gig using yesterday's strategies, you'll hurt your chances for visibility, engagement, and interviews. On the other hand, when your mindset says, "I'm willing to try some new ideas and ready to let go of past mistakes," you are on the right track. Here's how to create the referrals you need – and the mistakes you need to avoid – on your way to your next career move.

"I'm just not getting any traction with submitting my resumé or CV and filling out job applications," says just about everyone except the person whose resumé matches the job requirements exactly and verbatim. How can you get visibility, especially when no one is ever a 100% match for a job posting?

When jobs are scarce, finding opportunities means using the skills that we've been discussing in every chapter so far: adaptability and innovation.

So if your game plan is to just keep filling out applications and blasting your resumé or CV to anyone who can fog a mirror, I wonder: How's that working for you? Is spray and pray getting you the results you want?

Results, in a tight job market, come from referrals.

Referrals result from how effectively you differentiate yourself.

> **Vala Afshar** ✔
> @ValaAfshar
>
> Career advice:
>
> 1 you are not your job
> 2 I can > IQ
> 3 do not speak poorly about others
> 4 there is no career ladder
> 5 know when it is time to leave
> 6 you do not need a title to lead
> 7 always meet deadlines
> 8 deliver outside your job description
> 9 stay teachable
> 10 share the credit

Every day, everyone in a leadership role is on the receiving end of invitations to connect. It's crowded out there in the LinkedIn-o-sphere. Guess who's getting pinged all the time for connections: it's your dream boss. Your ideal mentor. Your future recruiter. Your next hiring manager. And your future investor. You'll need more than luck to beat the odds in the COVID-19 Connection Economy. You need a game plan. And you've got to understand how to share your "third dimension."

Your CV (resumé) and your LinkedIn profile are a two-dimensional picture of who you are. Or, more specifically, what you've done. Dates, stats, education. Important stuff – but never the whole story.

The third dimension is where your value proposition – and your values – come to life. The third dimension is an unexpected and welcome skill. The third dimension is something extra. It's the connection that you can share in a way that goes beyond your resumé. Because your talents come in a package (that's *you*), the third dimension is where your personality, values, and work ethic come into play. Here are ways to create a third dimension for your personal brand, right now:

- **Record a Short Video:** Share a story or anecdote that emphasizes something about you. Need a prompt or an idea? Here's one: "I'd like to tell you something that you can't read on my resumé..." Turn your phone around and shoot that video: see what story you can tell, in three minutes or less. Remember: practice makes perfect. It's great to do more than one take to ensure you show up at your best!

- **Make Your Mark:** Build an online presence that illustrates your abilities, your thought leadership, and even a portfolio of your work. If you are an artist, designer, or work in any creative field whatsoever, a portfolio site is a must. Here's an example: http://karenmangia.com.

- **Leave a Trail:** Tools like Instagram and Facebook make it easy to record videos and package your unique skill set into various forms. For example, when the world went into lockdown, I decided that I would turn my home into an "all-inclusive resort" on Facebook. Of course, it's not really an all-inclusive resort, but I had a lot of fun imagining what I would do if I had guests visiting me. On the day of the Kentucky Derby, for example, I rolled out some crazy hats, photographed myself in the "stands" (actually, the stairsteps on my back patio), and even awarded the winner (a blue sawhorse I named "Champion"). Ridiculous? Perhaps. Funny? I think so. People DM me all the time to ask if they can make reservations. Maybe you will visit my page and draw your own conclusions. There's more to me – and to you – than just work. We all have that third dimension. And finding a way to laugh, especially during these tough times, is a dimension I'm interested in exploring. How about you?

- **Get Clear on Your Values:** What really matters to you, when it comes to your work ethic, focus, and contribution? Your values are an important part of your third dimension. What do you care about, when it comes to culture? Service? Teamwork? Consider a story that illustrates your values – a story where you don't just say empty phrases like, "I really value integrity" or "Servant leadership is my strategy." Look at the stories that quickly and easily illustrate and share your values. Tell a story about how you put your values into action. Demonstrate competence and character in action; don't just talk about concepts and expect people to see you as a "high-energy team player" (what does that even mean?). Think actions, not adjectives. The action you're looking for? *Impact.* Maybe trustworthiness is part of your third dimension. Then what's the story that supports that characteristic – where did you earn someone's trust, and how, and why? Consider how your values made an impact for your team, your family, your organization. Then, put those values on your website, your blog, or your YouTube channel. Because clear values need to be shared – and that third dimension is what brings your skill set to life.

- **One Step at a Time:** Be focused in your approach, when it comes to outreach. Have you got a video you really like? Don't litter the internet with requests to watch it. That approach looks like you don't understand your audience. Or your value proposition. Or the way the internet works.

We've talked about being deliberate when working from home: don't change that strategy just because you think the job search is a "pure numbers game." True, your numbers matter, but quality is what matters most. Don't blast the world with your gifts; share them with the folks you know would benefit.

> Working from home is a tool for economic development. Smart companies (and municipalities) are using the new normal to create increased jobs and economic activity.
>
> * In Utah, 80% of the jobs are located in just four counties, but the Utah Rural Outlook Initiative is focused on bringing remote workers to the other 25 counties in the state. In 2019, remote jobs reduced unemployment by a full percentage point in a single year.
> * The Tulsa Remote Municipal Marketing program offers $10,000 incentive payments to people who would bring their jobs with them to areas of Oklahoma.
>
> The socio-economic impact is huge: when workers don't have to live in an urban center in order to contribute, workers and communities benefit from economic and social diversity, improved lifestyle choices, and more. Working from home is just good business!

What Not to Do

Who can afford to make mistakes when the job market is tight? Nobody. That's why it is shocking to see the following eight strangers – and one standout superstar – asking for connections and help. How often do you masquerade as one of these characters in your "click-to-connect" messages? Do you recognize anyone on this list?

- **Generic George:** He just wants a job. At my company. Or any company where I know people. If I would just introduce him. Or write a referral for him. Or "share his resume with the right people inside my company." Or meet, via Zoom, to "share expertise." I begin to imagine George copying and pasting thousands of similar invite requests, naively believing that it only takes one yes to get him to his dream job. Or to any job. *Generic George's fatal flaw? He fails to offer any specifics that would move the conversation forward. His third dimension falls flat, because he doesn't have one – he just has his hand out. He has confused me with a "bot," blindly making algorithm-based referrals. The upside to George? He never follows up.*

- **Social Sally:** In a world full of strangers, Sally sees future friends. She has done an immense amount of research about me before sending her message. She artfully works our shared hobbies into the thread. And quotes from my recent blogs. Sally comes across as familiar and engaging. And I always know I can count on her to follow up if I don't respond. Depending on the time of year, she may also send me a thoughtful birthday or work service anniversary acknowledgment. I start picturing Social Sally joining my book club. But not my company. *Social Sally's fatal flaw? Believing that being likable will get her the referral, the job, or the promotion. I want to have fun with Sally. But I have no idea why I would refer her, hire her, or promote her. Because she never tells me.*

- **Wandering Wally:** He's never met an idea he doesn't like. He's never had a thought he hasn't spoken. Every notion that hits his noggin connects to another random, unrelated idea and thought – which he can't wait to share. In fact, he can't help himself. Wandering Wally is all over the map. He wants to be an astronaut. He wants to save the world. He is currently patenting an invention. Despite his background as a CPA, he might be ready to cross over into a career in sales. And he puts this all in his first message to me, even though we've never met. I begin to picture Wally living in a house that is permanently being remodeled. By the end of his message, I am simultaneously exhilarated and exhausted. *Wandering Wally's fatal flaw? He lacks a clear, concise direction and message. He has confused me with a career counselor. And this message with a brainstorming session.*

- **Egomaniac Ethan:** He is the best there's ever been at everything he's ever done. And, thankfully, he's not too shy to share it! He is a top performer. He is already being recruited for numerous jobs but thought he would do me the favor of connecting with me. He was Prom King. He is into extreme sports. People tell him he smells good. And, he knows that everyone idolizes him. As evidenced by the 86 references he would be glad to share. Oh, wait a minute . . . yep, he already did. PS: I might be interested to know that he has some very important connections. After all, how many people have flown on a private plane with a billionaire to his private island? I start to flashback to bad 80s movies. And toxic teams. *Egomaniac Ethan's fatal flaw? His total lack of self-awareness. Trying to impress isn't the same as trying to connect. His confidence, when taken to the extreme, sends the signal that he will be a nightmare to manage. Instantly, I know I will jeopardize a relationship if I refer him to someone in my network.*

- **Desperado Diane:** She is a living, breathing country and western song (https://tinyurl.com/wfh-sadsongs). She would have invited me to connect sooner, but there's been a series of catastrophes. "Thank God, and Greyhound, He's Gone," Diane says, because "The Worst He Ever Gave Me Was the Best I Ever Had." The details of the tragedy include crying, loving, and leaving – a very familiar refrain. "Ever Since I Said 'I Do,' There's a Lot of Things He

Don't," she confesses, whether I want to hear it or not. But the good news is that she's put that all behind her now. And she welcomes me referring her to the most senior and experienced people in my network. *Desperado Diane's fatal flaw? Oversharing. And if she's like this with me during her first message, I don't want to hear the chorus.*

- **Mentor Me Mandy:** She starts strong. The tone of her message is conversational but not overly casual. She is prepared but not assumingly personal. She knows something about the job she's seeking and can reasonably articulate her strengths. Where does it go wrong? At the end of the message, Mandy does not ask for a job. Or for a referral. Or even for an introduction. Even though I'm already aware she wants at least one of the above. Instead, Mandy asks me to be her mentor. *Mentor Me Mandy's fatal flaw? Setting up a compelling story and then failing to make her real ask. And asking for a significant investment of time with no offer of a value exchange instead. Always have the courage to ask for what you want!*

- **Perpetual Pete:** He will reach out to you time and time again, asking for help getting a new job. His current job pays well, but there's not enough equity. His previous job had a ton of equity, but the compensation plan was less than competitive, so he bailed for a new paycheck. Perpetual Pete is a wanderer and is in need of finding his true purpose – something that can bring him joy beyond financial outcomes. *Perpetual Pete's fatal flaw? His only value is money. And he's a little too thirsty. It is hard to provide a strong reference for people who are driven by only financial reasons – they can often leave a trail of unfinished work and incomplete promises. Mercenaries don't make for good employees – or good referrals. Remember what Michelle Obama said: "Success isn't about how much money you make; it's about the difference you make in people's lives."*

- **Long-Lost Lisa:** A woman I worked with in 2002 reaches out to me and asks if I can help her to find a job at Salesforce. No reminders of how we worked together but she got the company name right. Aha! Yes, I remember her. Now, what was it that she wanted? *Long-Lost Lisa's fatal flaw? Showing up out of nowhere. Or out of desperation. Take your pick. There's no relevance, no message of today, no clues as to what she wants or what value she can bring. Relationships matter, but if your story isn't relevant and relatable to right now, I can't really help you!*

Fortunately, I occasionally hear from Powerhouse Pat. Who is Powerhouse Pat?

Powerhouse Pat is the standout superstar in a cast of mediocrity.

Pat is prepared.

Pat is articulate. Focused. Pat has clear priorities. Simple and precise talking points. Examples of outcomes and impact. A well-thought-out ask at the end of the message. And an offer of shared value or reciprocity. Powerhouse Pat is the one who gets the yes. The connection. The referral.

How can you show up as Powerhouse Pat and increase your odds of a successful outcome? Invest as much thought in crafting your click-to-connect message as you would in preparing for a job interview. Your message matters. Your message is your tool to make a great first impression. And to differentiate yourself.

Remember, the simplest message is always the strongest. Before you send your high-stakes click-to-connect referral request, be sure your invitation message concisely answers these four questions:

1. What differentiates me (and my message) from others?

2. What is the purpose of my connection request, and is my ask clear in the message?

3. Does this message come across as trustworthy? Have I represented myself accurately and provided examples that make the person on the receiving end more likely to engage?

4. Have I offered a way to return the favor or to create a value exchange?

Success begins with your story.

These are very difficult times for people who are looking for meaningful jobs and new career opportunities. Asking for a referral, and getting one, can seem like hard work. But it doesn't have to be, if you take the time to get clear on your value proposition. Consider your third dimension, and the value you can provide.

Because every employer, everywhere, is looking for solutions providers. What's your solution? What's your service? Maybe your industry has gone by the wayside, or your company is no longer in business. You may be out of work but you are not out of options.

Options always exist, even in a tough economy. Choices. Opportunities. Even if you haven't discovered them yet. If you think you've tried everything, you haven't. Here are some other guidelines to help you sort through your goals:

1. **Define Success:** Get specific about the outcome you aspire to achieve through and with your extended network. For example, are you seeking a new job? Career advice? Amplification of your content? An introduction to an influential thought leader? Clearly defining success narrows your field of focus to prospective contacts who can move you closer toward achieving your goals. Invest first in building networks of quality rather than quantity.

2. **The Power of Intention:** Once you develop a shortlist of people to connect with, do your homework. "Everyone

leaves a trail of crumbs behind on social media," explains Gurvinder Singh Sahni (https://www.linkedin.com/in /gurvindersahni/), CMO of Appirio (a Wipro company) (http://appirio.com, http://wipro.com). "Those crumbs provide invaluable insights about how to plan an effective first interaction. I've met some of my best business partners on Twitter first. And I've sourced keynote speakers for big events through Twitter that I've never met before as well. All because I did my homework to discover what we had in common. A single social media comment that's well thought out invites future connection and relationship."

3. **What's My Line?** *TV Guide* ranked *What's My Line?* in the top 10 television game shows of all time. The show ran on CBS for over 20 years, beginning in 1954. The premise was simple: celebrity panelists were blindfolded and a mystery guest would come into the studio. The whole idea was for the panelists to try and guess the occupation (the "line") of the guest. Governors, scientists, athletes, and celebrities brought an added element to the show, as panelists could only ask a series of yes or no questions. But finding out who someone really is, using just yes or no questions, is a difficult game! Are you using yes or no questions with your online networking and connection requests? "Avoid the, '*Can I pick your brain?*' and '*Could we get coffee or virtual coffee?*' requests," shares Sofia Rodriguez Mata (http:// www.linkedin.com/in/sofmata), Community Manager at Salesforce. She says that those questions obscure the true intention behind your connection request. Instead of asking a yes or no question, immediately establish trust and offer reciprocity. What could you do, share, or say that would have *value* for your contact? That's what reciprocity means. The value you offer is the service you can provide, the introductions you can make, the insight you can share. Then, be clear about what you want to discuss and what you want to gain: don't turn your career into a guessing

game. List the topics and your goals in the initial outreach. By the way, if you've got seven goals and five topics, don't celebrate that even dozen just yet. You've got too much on your plate! Simplify, simplify, simplify. Keep your initial contact brief, clear, and concise. You can close the request by discussing what you can offer in return. Most of the time, the receiver is impressed enough by the transparency of the message that they are happy to make time for you without cashing in on your reciprocity offer.

4. **Turn the Tables:** Before you click to comment or to connect, turn the tables on your own message. If you were on the receiving end of your own invitation, would you accept it? Is your message customized to the recipient? Is your objective, intention, or outcome clearly articulated? Have you been transparent about what you aspire to achieve and what you have to offer? If not, take a moment to revisit your message. Then look at it for a third time – because you're looking for the third dimension. What can you say that shows your values and personality without overdoing it? Would you be interested in hearing from you?

5. **Be the Change You Want to See:** Have you written a recommendation on LinkedIn today? Why not? I'm not talking about a double tap for a particular skill. I'm talking about taking a moment to craft a few well-chosen words around a colleague you respect. Don't tell them you're doing it, just do it. Select someone whose work you admire – someone you've worked with – and tell the world why this person is something special. The visibility is good for your network and theirs. The kind of person who writes an unsolicited recommendation is the kind of person who understands service, networking, connection . . . and karma.

6. **Curate Community:** If networking continually falls to the bottom of your to-do list, try creating a community. Create a connecting point for a network of networks to come together to form a community based on shared interests.

"Don't be afraid to put yourself out there in creative ways," says Sharon Klardie (http://linkedin.com/in/sharonklardie), Senior Manager of Salesforce Labs. "I started a virtual book club and host virtual #IAmRemarkable workshops. Taking these actions helps me stay connected and meet new people while making a positive impact on others as well. Plus, these communities scale impact." A quick way to connect with communities: joining LinkedIn groups. If you're serious about a job search, are you in one of the recruiter groups? Are you in groups that represent industries of interest, not just your own? You don't have to be a recruiter in order to connect with them. There are a myriad of groups on LinkedIn – places where you can go to find like-minded individuals as well as new opportunities. And, in the case of executive recruiters, the people who can help you to make your next move.

7. **Amplify Authentically:** From reposting content to referrals and recommendations, how you interact says more about you than written words. Are you commenting on posts that strike a chord? How do you share your perspective and your own thought leadership? Approach online comments as an extension of your personal reputation, values, and brand. Visibility is the goal that you gain when you share what matters most to you. How are you expressing that third dimension? Employers want to know!

Extending your network begins with defining your goals and solidifying your story. One resource to help you define and articulate what differentiates you, as well as construct a clear ask, is the *Success With Less* Career Companion (https://tinyurl.com/wfh-companion).

Consider what Tim Ferriss asked in his book *Tribe of Mentors* (Houghton Mifflin Harcourt 2017): What would it look like if this were easier?

Right now, maybe it's hard to imagine that "easier." I hear you. I get that. For many, this economy is tougher than the global financial crisis – maybe even tougher than the Great Depression.

But, no matter how tough it gets, you can't run out of imagination. What if you used a little on your career? What if some imagination made things easier?

What if you opened up your mind to the first two words of this sentence:

What if?

The first step to creating new possibilities is imagining that possibilities exist. If your mindset says you're out of options, how can you take action? If you've been trying and working and striving to find that next job, but nothing's breaking loose, you're probably pretty frustrated right now.

But does that mean that success doesn't exist? Or that it's just not on your timeline? It's your choice how you move forward. How can you change your approach to find new options for yourself? Start with the way you enter the referral and networking conversation. Here's why:

When you change your conversation, you change your results.

Isn't that the shift that your career needs?

> **Vala Afshar** ✓
> @ValaAfshar
>
> 10 things to quit right now:
>
> 1 a sense of entitlement
> 2 speaking poorly behind someone's back
> 3 constantly complaining
> 4 resentment
> 5 making excuses
> 6 worrying about the past
> 7 interrupting people
> 8 bragging about being busy
> 9 fishing for compliments
> 10 settling for mediocrity

The Climb

"**C**ome on, you can do it!"

I was cheering. Standing on the side of a mountain and cheering.

"You've got this!" I called out to the stranger, 30 feet in front of me. She was frozen in place. I started to clap. "Don't even look down! You're going to be fine! You're halfway there! Woo hoo!"

The Flatiron Mountains in Colorado are beautiful in the spring. My boyfriend Eric and I had decided to go hiking into the majestic wilderness outside of Boulder. Now, if you know me at all, you know that I'm not exactly the outdoorsy, athletic type. But I'm always up for an adventure and seeing something fantastic. So, we asked the park ranger what the best way was to see what was up there, as we pointed at the mountain.

We decided to go up the steeper side – the one that wasn't the beginner path – in spite of the ranger's cautions. Along the way, we met up with another couple. We joined forces, hiking together up the ridge. We met up on a flat path but soon it got steeper, and the altitude started taking our breath away as we saw the wide flat trail get thinner, tighter, and more treacherous. We got to a point that's about halfway through the hike, and that's when things got real.

An athletic guy who probably only shops at REI takes off across a narrow ledge. Looks like the ledge is about the width of your laptop, overlooking a steep overhang. How steep, I'm not sure, because I can't see the entirety of this patch of mountain. But as he dances across the ledge I see and hear tiny rocks and stones, dislodged from his footsteps, careening down the mountainside. Next up is his girlfriend. She starts strong but gets stuck midway.

She's the woman I'm yelling at because she is frozen on the ledge, unable to move. "This is awesome! You've got this!" I don't even know her, but my voice is declaring that I know she can do it. From the other side, across the ledge, her boyfriend is saying in a firm but calm tone, "Follow my voice. Follow my voice. You can do it..."

But she's barely moving, and she's got her arms spread out because she's trying to hug the mountain. Turns out, she's standing in an area of the ledge that's not as wide as your laptop.

It's about as wide as your iPad.

Actually, your iPad mini. Turned sideways.

Yes, it's true: Colorado really will take your breath away.

Somehow, she manages to get past her fear and hot steps it over to her boyfriend in a rush of adrenaline and survival instinct, and her man catches her as she bursts into tears. "It's okay! You made it!" I'm yelling at her. Just trying to keep it positive, right?

Eric takes off and goes across without too much trouble. I'm the last one. Now it's my turn.

I take two steps on the ledge. That's all I needed. I hear myself say, "*Oh ... hell no.*"

At this point, there's no one clapping for me, because if there were, I would have punched them.

What I didn't realize (until I got going) was that the ledge is littered with tiny pebbles and rocks. And as I'm stepping just two steps onto the rocks these pebbles are falling and squishing beneath my shoes and my footing is feeling very unstable but I'm trying to do the best I can and before I know it I'm standing on the iPad mini section of the mountain and I can't move.

Or breathe.

Because I look down from the midpoint of the ledge – it was hidden from my view until I got out there – to see just how far those little rocks and pebbles were falling. I am certain I am going to join them.

Eric's on the other side of the ledge and he calls back to me, asking if I want to turn around and go back. Go back? Either way, I still have to climb off of these rocks!

I'm starting to wonder what my options are for being air-lifted off the mountain.

I assume the same open-arms posture I had seen just moments before, leaning in toward the mountain. My inclination is to just get smaller and smaller and lean closer toward the sheer rocks in front of my face. I had to find my footing, and I'm taking the tiniest steps I can as Eric is calling out to me, in a firm but calm tone, "Follow my voice . . . you've got this . . ." Now where have I heard that before?

There's something interesting that happens when everything is uncertain – when everything is shifting and you feel like you can't find your footing and you know you can't turn back. At that moment, it didn't matter that I had successfully hiked Rocky Mountain National Park just two days earlier. It didn't matter that I had gotten a promotion six weeks ago or that I had helped mentor 25 new hires last year. The only context that mattered? The context of the mountain.

Small steps. Small steps are the key. If you're reading this, you know that I made it – and I did it one step at a time. I stopped cheering when I got a personal experience of why that ledge was so scary. Because I was on it, too.

It's so easy to start telling other people that "they can do it"! I'm a positive person, and I always will be there to cheer people to new results. I'm looking for reasons to celebrate people and what they can accomplish.

But the mountain and I had a moment.

Yes, encouragement is still important to me – people need to be reminded what they are capable of. But when encouragement comes from a place of truth and authenticity, it's much more meaningful than some motivational shouting or well-intentioned applause. On that mountainside, encouragement changed for me.

What happens when being positive isn't helping anybody – because you see that you're right there, on that same ledge, trying to find the courage to just put one foot in front of the other?

It's so easy to say, "Oh, that's not so tough! Just don't worry about it! Stay positive!" but it's also completely ineffective. That's according to Dr. Susan David (https://tinyurl.com/wfh-susandavid). In her book, *Emotional Agility: Get Unstuck, Embrace Change and Thrive in Work and Life* (Penguin, 2017), she shares that there's something more powerful than positivity. In an interview with the *Washington Post*, she says that "if we try to push away thoughts and emotions they will come back magnified." Psychologists call this *leakage*, she explains. We've created a culture of avoidance – trying to replace negative thoughts with positive ones. Turns out, those negative thoughts come back with a vengeance. Dr. David advocates for a different mindset.

"Emotional agility is a skillset that builds on our ability to face our emotions, to face them and move forward deliberately," Dr. David explains. "It's the ability to recognize when you're feeling stressed, be able to step out of your stress and then decide how to act in a way that is congruent with your personal values and goals."

For me on that mountain, I wasn't just stressed. I was terrified. I felt like I was in over my head. But I knew I had a goal: don't die. Get to the other side. Put one foot in front of the other.

Today, we are all on the side of a mountain, wondering what's next. How do we step beyond positive thinking to find a mindful and clear way to move forward? We have to understand our context, and our values, if we're going to make the climb.

And leaders have to have a crystal-clear vision: a vision of how we're going to manage our way off this mountain.

Over the past two decades, Gallup has studied performance at hundreds of organizations and measured the engagement of 27 million employees. Managers account for at least 70% of variance in employee engagement scores across business units, Gallup estimates in this report (https://tinyurl.com/wfh -gallup1).

In a study conducted by Ultimate Software and the Center for Generational Kinetics, 80% of employees think they can do their jobs without their managers (https://tinyurl.com /wfh-software). Get this: 80% also say their managers aren't necessary. Is that surprising, when less than half of managers report having a mentor that gives them guidance on how to be a better leader, and 45% have *never* received formal management training?

A Gallup study of over 7,000 Americans concluded that one out of every two people had actually left a job at some point during their career to get away from their managers in order to improve their overall quality of life.

Gallup's research suggests that about one in 10 people possess the talent to manage. That's why companies miss the mark on 82% of their management hiring decisions. Though many people are endowed with some of the necessary traits required for management, few have the unique combination of talent needed to help a team achieve excellence in a way that significantly improves a company's performance. Here's the good news: effective training can triple that statistic, providing you with three times as many qualified and effective managers.

The five qualities of effective managers:

1. They **motivate** – they create an engaging and compelling vision for employees.
2. They are **assertive** – driving outcomes and overcoming resistance.
3. They understand **accountability** – holding people to a higher standard.
4. They build **relationships** – based on trust, empathy, and open dialogue.
5. They are **decisive** – able to make decisions based on productivity, not politics.

Management talent could be hiding in plain sight. Your most talented managers might be underperforming right in front of your face. But there's an obstacle, challenge, or issue that you haven't discovered. So how can you find what's missing?

Seth Mattison (https://www.sethmattison.com/) is a specialist in workplace behavior – specifically, the kind of behavior that helps organizations to thrive. He commissioned a survey called "Leading the Leaders – Leading from Home." With 1,850 respondents, all managers and directors working remotely, at companies of 5,000 employees or more, the survey explores what the mid-level managers care about most of all. The survey measured 436 metrics on values, wants, needs, and expectations.

"Three interesting things emerged from the data," Seth says, from his office in LA, where he's sporting a gray Dodgers baseball cap and an Indiana University sweatshirt – a nod to both his current address and his Midwestern roots (he played football for a Division III school in Wisconsin). "We wanted to know what employees value most from the leaders and companies they work for. Relationships – a sense of belonging – came in at the very top. How we think about belonging is rooted in psychological safety. People want to know, 'Can I be me with this group?'" Seth says.

Leaders, however, often find themselves in a place where they have to forgo the value of belonging, because they have to stand out from the crowd and make difficult decisions. "It's not that they don't value acceptance," Seth explains, "but sometimes they have to do things that might not be universally agreed upon." So, how do we lean into this value system of relationships, acceptance, and belonging when we can no longer physically be with people? How can managers make the necessary tough calls while fostering an environment of engagement, support, and participation – when people aren't sharing the same space?

"When leadership makes it okay to be yourself," Seth explains, "that's the first step. Something as simple as a dog barking or kid popping into your office: that needs to be okay." Keeping your camera on is just good business for everybody, Seth says. Even though it might feel a little invasive at first, it's critical to building rapport on the team. Because, when people can't see you, it's easy to fall into the natural human trap of creating a story. Seth says the mind game goes something like this, when cameras are off: "Oh, he's distracted. She's doing something else. Maybe email? They aren't listening. He didn't like my point, I bet. That person had a problem with me when we were physically in the office and now we're working remotely and they are still blowing me off and running their political game. Whatever."

Managers have to ask more questions in the new normal. When it's okay to be yourself, it's okay to make the tough calls, too. That's part of the job. Meanwhile, managers have to be on the lookout in the virtual world: looking for the natural human urge to fill in the blanks and make up stories when cameras are off. Those fill-in-the-blank stories lead to a lack of engagement, a lack of collaboration, and a counterculture narrative that can be very destructive in the remote workforce.

The second value that Seth discovered was the idea of ownership. Personal responsibility is surging in the work-from-home world, as managers understand that empowering greater ownership is the key to distributed impact.

Ownership – knowing what needs to be done and then being responsible for making it happen – is tied directly to security. Security was another value that emerged as a subset – and why wouldn't it? The pandemic has created more uncertainty and insecurity than we've seen since World War II, maybe even more in some sectors. And security links to the third key value: acknowledgment and visibility. In his work, Seth discovered that 89% of remote workers wish that they had more acknowledgment. "People are worried that they're not being seen," Seth says. "It's interesting how my CEO clients say that productivity, right now, is going through the roof. Of course it is," Seth says with a slight chuckle. "Engagement went up in the USA in 2009–2010, coming out of the recession. One of the reasons for increased engagement – then and now – is that people are just grateful to have a job." Gratitude is great, but the sustainable approach focuses on *connection*.

"It's unrealistic to think that you're going to take a disengaged team from the office and then turn them into remote workers and their performance and engagement will improve. But one of our clients has designed meetings to build deeper engagement and ownership into their approach. Every week, someone on the team is responsible for 5–10 minutes of guidance on something they've learned, studied, or discovered." It's a mini-mastermind for mid-level managers. "The team leveled up, as people started taking greater ownership and looking in the direction of service and insights," Seth says.

What every manager has to do in the distributed work environment is easy to describe but hard to do. "Be present," Seth says, simply. But what exactly does that mean? "Bring the power of your presence to the individuals on your team. It's so easy to get lost in the 'bam-boom, three-minute Zoom' world, where we're juggling emails, texts, and telephone calls. But if you're just going through the motions – connecting with employees like you're dealing with a punch list and checking the boxes while your head is somewhere else, people know it."

Managers: set up more time than you need for check-in conversations. Seth explains, "You've got to have space to demonstrate caring, right now. You have to show up with clear communication around expectations. Crystal-clear outcomes and accountability, these things are more important than ever." Indeed, if you want greater ownership, and employees seek security and belonging, tell them exactly what you want them to own and link it to what they value. "That 'knowingness' helps reduce a team member's anxiety. It helps folks to know where they stand. Where they're going. What you need. As a leader, wholehearted communication is where it all begins," according to Seth. That wholehearted leadership, in a remote work environment, isn't easy. Because that kind of impact means you have to eliminate distractions.

Distraction is the new dismissiveness. And it's deadly for managers. Give your team members your undivided attention. Let them know that they are visible and acknowledged. Distraction drives disengagement. People want to feel important; paying attention to your team is the most powerful way you can share your presence.

And that presence begins with listening.

Seth explains, "What we know about great leadership, about high-performing teams, about engagement, about relationships . . . it is all still there. We don't have to reinvent this whole new world," he says. We just have to think about how we deliver and execute within it.

What is it that you need to discover about your team, your managers, your employees? Share your executive presence in the most powerful way you can: listen. Share these three powerful words in a way that's authentic and demonstrated in action: "I hear you."

If your team hasn't been trained in listening skills, you might want to consider how that "soft skill" turns into hard results in a distributed workforce. Top managers understand how to hear what they need to know, acknowledging where employees are, and sharing guidance from a more informed place. Because understanding a new perspective always influences our own.

That's not to say that acknowledgment is agreement. Visibility isn't just an opportunity to grant wishes. Not all conversations lead to a pay raise, or a four-day workweek, or whatever other requests might come your way. Whether the ultimate decision is yes or no, leaders understand that connection comes from a listening that says, I see where you are coming from. Without that connection, you can't expect ownership, engagement, or impact. All you'll get is compliance – and sometimes, not even that.

Listening opens up the dialogue to collaborative leadership. It's no surprise that the *Harvard Business Review* says that over 67% of managers are uncomfortable communicating with employees for any reason (https://tinyurl.com/wfh-hbr1). We weren't very good at processing performance reviews and corrective action before COVID-19. What is going to make it better and reverse that trend? We haven't been taught how to listen, and how to lead, in a way that's constructive. How does your team show up when it's time to process negative feedback?

A new kind of presence, with fresh management skills, is what's needed. Now more than ever, wholehearted leadership begins with listening. Listening is a critical-path requirement in the new normal.

The kind of listening that rests on the power of these three words: *I hear you.*

Beyond conversational skills, listening hinges on your organization's ability to gather and measure data, insights and behavior.

- Does your team know the right questions to ask to drive engagement, discover challenges, and encourage transparency?
- Do you have the measurement tools in place so that you can go beyond the survey in evaluating your remote workforce?
- Are you really listening to your customers, helping them to identify and overcome challenges? After all, aren't your customers an extension of your organization?
- How do you share these three words, through your managers and with your entire team: "I hear you"?

It's no coincidence that the title of my next book is *Listen Up!* As Vice President of Customer & Market Insights for Salesforce, I've built my career on learning how to turn listening into a competitive advantage. If you're interested, I'd like to do the same for you. There's more to be explored regarding what active listening really means, including the technology and tools that enable organizations to succeed. If you're curious about harnessing the power inside of your organization, I hope you will check it out. Details can be found on my website, http://karenmangia.com.

Reach into your organization to find the way forward. Listen to what people need. Help your managers and your customers and your entire team to align with a set of values that build on transparency, trust, and collaboration. Be wise enough to know that when you have a thought or a feeling, it doesn't mean that it's right or that you have to act on it. After all, just because a train of thought shows up it doesn't mean you have to ride it.

Working from home and managing a remote workforce can be scary. You might feel unsure of your footing. You might feel like you are in unfamiliar territory. Welcome to the shift. We're all on the same mountain. The great news is that there are some amazing discoveries to be made, inside the new normal. You've made it this far and there's no turning back.

It's not just positive thinking that lets me know you can move forward. It's because I've moved forward, too. I've reinvented. I've innovated. I made it off that mountain. I've found new ways of delivering value from inside my home office. And I know how human nature works. We always find a way forward. Innovation is built into the system. We have the ability to be more than what we fear. We have the ability to embrace this shift, and all that it entails, so that we can find what's next.

Where you are is not who you are. You can be you from anywhere. Productivity isn't a place, it's an outcome. What are the outcomes you want for yourself, your company, your career? Success is waiting for you – maybe even right there at your kitchen table. Or inside a diary. Or written in a note from a child.

And if you find yourself feeling uncertain on a steep mountainside, or inside your home office, slow down for a moment. There is a way forward. You'll find it, even in unfamiliar territory. Keep looking. Keep going. One step at a time: that's how you make the climb.

Acknowledgments

*W*orking from Home: Making the New Normal Work for You exemplifies what's possible when innovation, collaboration, and opportunity intersect. What started as a blog became a book in the span of less than three months because so many talented people were willing to explore the answer to, "Why not?"

Thank you to James Hinchcliffe for sharing your deeply personal journey from setback to comeback. On or off the racetrack, you will always be a winner in my book. Literally and figuratively. Your humility and kindness are what we need more of in the world.

Thank you to Bruce Richardson for convening the weekly Virtual Social Coffee Hour that created this collaboration opportunity. And for pulling out all the stops to bring this book to life in the span of a few months while still asking me about my plans for the weekend (as if I had any).

I'm deeply grateful to Vala Afshar for raising the bar on how to make an impact in a new context and for inviting me to join you. Great leaders ask great questions, and "Would you like to blog about Work from Home?" changed the trajectory of my career for the better.

John Taschek, you lead the Dream Team. And I'm grateful to be a part of your team and for your thoughtful contribution to the blog series and to this book. You make space for all of us to explore, discover, and become our own best.

Thank you to Dan Farber and to David Simon for paving a path to success for this story. And to my Salesforce Ohana @ Home Task Force colleagues who generously share your wisdom and challenge me to up my home office game: Jennifer Betowt, Wally Bruner, Rick Gyan, Charlie Isaacs, Sharon Klardie, Jody Kohner, Kirstyn Levine, Amanda Nelson, Elizabeth Pinkham, and Paul Wilhoit.

I'm grateful that Chris Westfall is always up for an adventure. Because the journey from contract to manuscript in 35 days is a bumpy, wild ride with hairpin turns and no time for scenic selfies. When presented with said adventure, I'm thrilled your response was, "This makes way too much sense." Thanks for sharing your genius, your connections, and your creativity. You helped transform this story into something more cohesive and compelling than a "collection of blogs." My thanks to LGG and the VP of Operations for their support as well.

The team at Wiley is filled with magic makers and miracle workers. Thank you to Jeanenne Ray, Sally Baker, Dawn Kilgore, and the entire team for delivering what others deemed impossible. We built a sports car together while flying an airplane, and we laughed in the face of danger. I'll always look back on this time through rose-colored glasses because of you. To Tami and Missy at Cape Cod Editors: when we asked if you could edit as we go, you said yes. We couldn't have hit our timeline without you. Thanks for your excellent editing skills!

Thank you to the companies and subject matter experts who trusted me with your stories:

Vala Afshar at Salesforce; Bari Baumgardner at SAGE Event Management; Kevin Collins at Accenture; Joseph Davey at Vine & Table; Laura Farrer at Distribute Consulting; Patty Hatter & Rick Garza at Palo Alto Networks; Sharon Klardie at Salesforce; Khushali Kohli of KSAI Consulting; Andrew Lannerd at Transcendent Travel; James Loduca at Twitter; Seth Mattison at FutureSight Labs; Jack and Patricia Moore at Johnson Space Center; Keisha Nickolson at Pike Township Metropolitan School District; Gurvinder Singh Sahni at Apprio; Jill Snyder at Big Red Liquors; and Sofia Rodriguez Mata at Salesforce. I owe a debt of gratitude to Brant Pinvidic whose expertise proved invaluable in shaping the leading practices shared. And for giving me the "Director's Cut" on how to tell a successful story in print. Thank you to David Hicks and Seema Kohli of TribeCX for brainstorming, sharing research, and introducing me to your network of experts.

Lorelei, Piper, and Brynn, when you wrote me that box of motivational letters, you had no idea I would need to ration them across two books (neither did I). I keep your letters in plain sight on my desk, because you remind me that hope, encouragement, and cheer are always a glance away. And that success is always about where you fix your focus. You bring so much joy to my life everyday. Let's celebrate this book with Italian food!

Thank you to my Aunt Lucia for keeping my grandmother alive through sharing her diaries and her demeanor. Part of her lives on through you, for which I am incredibly grateful. Thank you to my mother for her support and encouragement in a myriad of ways as this manuscript unfolded.

It's been said that a friend in need is a friend indeed. And that's why I'm deeply indebted to Andrew for lending your creative skills and attending to every detail of bringing this book to market with style and aplomb. This trip has been a bigger one than many others we've taken around the world together. And to John, Michael, Sweet T, BDJ, Jill, Craig, Tonya, Moni, Suzannah, and Kara for cheering me on when I doubted and faltered.

Eric, this book literally would not have been without your encouragement. When I talked myself out of writing it, you steadfastly said, "You have to do this!" And you never wavered. You sacrificed relaxing dinners in favor of book brainstorming sessions, even after your own long days at work. And you gave me permission to get lost in thought, oftentimes mid-sentence. Thank you for being so supportive.

Finally, to all my readers. I wrote this story to invite you to step out of your sweatpants and into success. And to illuminate a path from your home office to the corner office without ever changing your commute. We are learning together, and I'm excited to discover how you are making work from home work for you.

KM

http://karenmangia.com

About the Author

Karen Mangia is Vice President, Customer and Market Insights at Salesforce where she engages current and future customers around the world to discover new ways of creating success and growth together. She has been featured in *Forbes* and regularly writes for ZDNet as well as for over 50,000 employees of Salesforce – an ecosystem that reaches over 3 million people worldwide. She also serves on the company's Racial Equality and Justice Task Force. She is a TEDx speaker and regularly delivers keynotes to thousands of managers and C-suite leaders across the globe.

Karen is a trained chef and is probably cooking something fabulous right now, if she's not working on a virtual keynote presentation.

Her next book, *Listen Up!*, will be released from Wiley in October of 2020.

Twitter: @karenmangia

Linkedin: http://www.linkedin.com/in/karenmangia

https://tinyurl.com/wfh-listenup

Index